Forensic Psychiatry Made Easy for Psychiatrist. A Practical Guide for Psychiatrists, Trainees, and Mental Health Professionals

For information, contact:

Saleh Ahmed Ali Alghamdi
Psychiatry Department, College of Medicine
Imam Mohammad Ibn Saud Islamic University (IMSIU)
Riyadh, Saudi Arabia

SAAlghamedi@imamu.edu.sa

First Edition: 2025

ISBN: 979-8-9930315-1-4

PREFACE

Preface by Professor Gary A. Chaimowitz

Head of Forensic Psychiatry, St. Joseph's Healthcare Hamilton, Canada | Professor, McMaster University, Academic Division Head, Hamilton, Canada

Forensic psychiatry is situated at the crossroads of medicine, law, and society. Its practitioners are usually called upon to make life-changing decisions whose implications extend beyond the patients they assess, treat and manage. The implications of their work extend well into the legal system and the safety of the general population. The publication of this book comes at a time when the world over there has been an increasing demand for readily available materials that are reliable and practical for use in the training of forensic psychiatrists and other mental health professionals interacting with the legal system.

Forensic Psychiatry Made Easy arrives at a pivotal moment in the evolution of forensic mental health practices worldwide. With clarity, precision, and relevance, this book addresses major areas that professionals encounter in practical forensic contexts, including criminal responsibility, risk assessment, civil competencies, and expert testimony. The step-by-step and structured approach evidenced in this book is accessible and evidence based and is also grounded in ethical reasoning and clinical experience.

The outstanding quality of this work is such that it is both accessible to trainees and substantial enough for experienced practitioners. It is not only academically grounded and articulates principles, but also practical considerations, case illustrations, and even structured templates that can directly aid practice. It also highlights a crucial fact: forensic psychiatry is as much about the individual before us as it is about the law.

I would like to congratulate Dr. Saleh Alghamdi on this important project and on providing a resource that is sure to lead to higher standards, increased clarity, and improved outcomes in a variety of forensic psychiatry contexts.

Preface by Dr. Mohammed Aljaffer

Forensic psychiatry stands at a unique intersection between medicine and law. It requires not only advanced clinical expertise but also a deep understanding of legal systems, ethical considerations, and the ability to communicate psychiatric opinions with clarity and precision within judicial settings. The role of the forensic psychiatrist extends beyond patient care to advising courts, supporting justice, and contributing to public safety.

In Saudi Arabia, interest in forensic psychiatry is growing. However, the number of officially qualified forensic psychiatrists remains extremely limited — currently fewer than the fingers on both hands. This scarcity highlights both the challenges and the urgency of developing specialized training pathways, fostering expertise, and creating high-quality educational resources tailored to our legal, cultural, and healthcare systems.

Forensic Psychiatry Made Easy was written to help address this critical gap. The book simplifies complex forensic principles, presenting them in a clear, systematic, and academically rigorous manner. Each chapter builds upon the previous, guiding readers through the essential aspects of contemporary forensic psychiatric practice. Case studies, structured assessments, and real-world examples make the material highly applicable to daily clinical and legal work.

As a Saudi forensic psychiatrist, I am both proud and hopeful to witness the growing interest among young doctors in this vital subspecialty. This book represents an important step toward building local expertise that is firmly grounded in international standards while remaining sensitive to the specificities of our legal and cultural context.

I extend my sincere congratulations to Dr. Alghamdi, who is among the very few - and almost the third person in Saudi Arabia - to have received specialized training in forensic psychiatry, for producing this timely and valuable resource. I am confident that Forensic Psychiatry Made Easy will serve as a cornerstone reference for the education and development of current and future generations of Saudi forensic psychiatrists, contributing meaningfully to the advancement of forensic mental health in our region.

Dr. Mohammed Abdullah Aljaffer

Associate Professor and Consultant of Forensic, Psychosomatic Medicine and Neuropsychiatry
College of Medicine - King Saud University.

ACKNOWLEDGEMENT

The process of writing this book has been both personal and professional, and I owe a massive debt of gratitude to everyone who helped me along the way.

Primarily, I would like to thank Professor Gary Chaimowitz of McMaster University. Being my previous supervisor and mentor, he has had a significant influence on my attitude towards forensic psychiatry. I am still inspired by his advice, philanthropy, and educational dedication. It is my privilege that he has consented to provide a preface to this work. I would also like to express my gratitude to Dr. Mohammed Aljaffer, an Assistant Professor of psychiatry at King Saud University, whose exceptional enthusiasm and creativity have been a source of inspiration for me. His practical assistance and insightful comments highlight the increasing impact of forensic psychiatry in Saudi Arabia.

I would also like to acknowledge my colleagues, trainees, and mentors who have helped me learn about forensic psychiatric practice by working with me, discussing their experiences, and sharing their insights. I would particularly like to thank the numerous patients whose cases have prompted me to think more critically about ethics, law, and clinical care.

I would like to express my sincere gratitude to my family, particularly my parents, my wife "Wardah", my kids and close friends, who have supported me in this endeavor and demonstrated patience and faith in the value of this work.

Lastly, I would like to acknowledge the broader forensic psychiatry community, both locally and internationally, for its efforts to elevate standards of care, education, and justice. I hope that this book will play, in some small part, its role in that common endeavor.

With deepest gratitude,

Saleh Ahmed Ali Alghamdi

Table of Contents

Chapter One: Introduction

Forensic psychiatry is an expanding branch of psychiatry associated with legislation and mental health. It is essential to evaluate the individuals involved in legal issues and provide opinions to the courts. Criminal and civil subjects are used for assessment, while treatment is less emphasized in forensic psychiatry than in general psychiatry. These are the issues of criminal responsibility, competency assessment, and risk assessment. The field is relatively new in certain countries, and most psychiatrists in these countries have little experience conducting legal assessments. The above is especially so since several courts ask for a psychiatric evaluation in varying levels of formality. These, nevertheless, constitute materials that give useful, culturally appropriate information for psychiatrists and trainees in law-related contexts. Every chapter introduces concepts, ethical standards, and workers' roles. It is to increase confidence, improve the quality of forensic assessment, and apply mental health knowledge in the legal system without violating medical and cultural standards.

1.1 Definition and Scope of Forensic Psychiatry

Forensic psychiatry is a medical subspecialty that applies psychiatric knowledge to legal questions. It addresses criminal and civil legal systems by providing mental health evaluations relevant to legal decisions(Arboleda-Florez, 2006). These evaluations include assessments of criminal responsibility, competency to stand trial, risk of violence, and civil capacities such as the ability to make medical decisions, write a will, or manage finances. Forensic psychiatry focuses on the interface between psychiatry and the law, often involving individuals who may not be seeking care voluntarily.

Forensic psychiatrists work in various situations as evaluators and clinicians. In an evaluative capacity, they offer expert opinions to courts or legal authorities. Their evaluations are objective and follow strict legal standards. In a clinical capacity, they may provide mental health care to incarcerated individuals or those in secure hospitals(Arboleda-Florez, 2006). Correctional psychiatry is often included within forensic psychiatry, as it involves diagnosing and managing mental illness in prison populations.

Although general psychiatrists deal with mental health, forensic psychiatrists specialize in understanding how psychiatric conditions relate to legal systems and procedures. The information in their reports can significantly influence decisions on personal freedom or legal entitlements(Kennedy, 2021). In many developing countries, the introduction of legal reforms and increased acceptance of mental illness by society have increased the demand for psychiatric skills for courts, police, and prisons. Similarly, an urgent need is to ensure robust training in forensic psychiatry in areas where the provision of mental health services is at the developing stages(Kennedy, 2021). Due to the lack of intense training and practice infrastructure, there is a scattered model of forensic psychiatry. Therefore, specialists and trainees must anticipate the competencies and roles of forensic psychiatry.

The role of forensic psychiatrists extends beyond deciding patients' mental states. One of their main functions is to provide psychiatric information in a language that legal practitioners understand. It requires a thorough knowledge of national legal systems and standard practices for the care of patients with mental disorders.

Forensic psychiatry involves knowledge of mental disorders, legal responsibility, professional and legal ethics, and organizational norms. It is a specialized practice area requiring expertise in psychiatry and law. Thus, forensic psychiatrists can afford justice while respecting the rights of mentally ill persons by observing structured training, practical guidelines, and ethical awareness.

1.2 Historical Context

The history of forensic psychiatry dates back to the time when the legal systems started to realize that mental illness may be a factor in crime and punishment. The first documented case is James Hadfield, born in England in 1800 (Gutheil, 2005). Hadfield tried to kill King George III but was acquitted on the grounds of insanity. This action led to the enactment of the Criminal Lunatics Act of 1800 and later to the formulation of the M'Naghten Rules in 1843, which defined legal insanity in standard law systems. These rules remain in force in many countries regarding the defense of insanity.

In the 19th century, psychiatry became more institutionalized, and its application to legal issues expanded. Physicians such as Philippe Pinel in France and Benjamin Rush in the United States contributed to early ideas about mental illness and criminal behavior. In the early 20th century, forensic psychiatry developed as a distinct subspecialty in North America and parts of Europe. Institutions such as Broadmoor Hospital in the UK and forensic units in the United States began treating mentally ill offenders separately from the general prison population.

By the mid-20th century, formal forensic psychiatry training programs emerged in Western countries. The American Board of Psychiatry and Neurology officially recognized forensic psychiatry as a subspecialty in 1992 (Stein et al., 2022). It led to the creation of structured fellowship programs, certification exams, and professional organizations such as the American Academy of Psychiatry and the Law (AAPL). These developments contributed to more straightforward guidelines, ethical standards, and legal credibility for forensic psychiatric practice.

In many countries, particularly those with developing mental health systems, forensic psychiatry is still in the process of development due to the increasing demand for psychiatric knowledge in the legal field. In such countries, the field is still in its infancy, and until the twentieth century, mental illness was treated through social and religious models rather than through forensic evaluation. While some parts of the world have made progress in adopting Western psychiatry models in legal systems, many still lack formal training programs in forensic psychiatry.

In various contexts, psychiatrists who studied abroad have incorporated forensic concepts into clinical and legal systems and have been involved in developing forensic services and clarifying mental illness and legal responsibility. However, forensic psychiatry still does not receive the attention it deserves in some national health care and legal systems, which hinders its ability to enhance legal processes in cases of mental disorders (Candilis& Martinez, 2021). The field requires educational programs, ethical standards, and motivational support to advance its development. The worldwide expansion of forensic psychiatry occurs because it combines legal and medical aspects with ethical and cultural considerations.

1.3 Core Functions and Subspecialties

Forensic psychiatry includes many practical activities supporting legal processes, judicial systems, and prisons. Major categories include criminal, civil, correctional psychiatry, and administrative evaluations. Various legal issues are evaluated in every area, requiring a considerable understanding of psychiatric evaluations, legal requirements, and ethical rationalization.

Criminal forensic assessments frequently require psychiatrists to decide if those accused of crimes qualify legally as sane when committing the crime and competent to engage in the court process. Criminal responsibility determinations determine whether the accused knew they were doing something criminal(Candilis& Martinez, 2021). In contrast, competency to stand trial assessments focus on the defendant's ability to understand legal procedures and to function productively with a lawyer. Forensic assessments should rely on formal interviews, pertinent background, and legal criteria in that law segment.

In the civil forensic world of assessment, psychiatrists examine the mental health aspects of testamentary capacity, guardianship needs, and suitability to parent. This type of assessment often involves aging adults with dementia or those whose mental illness has developed over time(Cerny-Suelzer et al., 2024). The psychiatrist should verify whether a person can reason, value, and apply vital facts. Special mention should be made of the evaluations of informed consent for medical interventions (when complicated treatments or psychiatric hospitalizations are involved).

The second important sphere is correctional psychiatry. In correctional settings, psychiatrists are available to treat various forms of mental illnesses, including mood disorders, psychosis, as well as a wide range of personality disorders, for inmates. Also, they evaluate the probability of suicide, provide medications, and provide assistance in dealing with acute behavioral problems. Correctional psychiatrists encounter difficulties in delivering care in settings defined by resources, physical dangers, and ethical tensions between offering aid and confining(Cerny-Suelzer et al., 2024). Despite the momentum in expanding correctional psychiatry, further work must be done to develop consistent guidelines, and enough trained personnel are needed.

Such an assessment measures whether one of the people is suitable for a job, whether the person can also perform the job safely, or whether they are qualified to receive a disability allowance. For example, a psychiatrist may decide whether a police officer's post-traumatic stress disorder (PTSD) has made him fit to return to work. Such assessments rely on reasoning out mental health problems and occupational standards(Martone, 2022). Moreover, such assessments are essential as part of military psychiatry and employee assistance programs.

Each forensic area has unique documentation standards. Reports must be clear, objective, and structured to answer specific legal questions. They must also avoid speculation, maintain neutrality, and be understandable to non-psychiatric readers(Martone, 2022). Well-written forensic reports are critical for ensuring that experts correctly use psychiatric opinions in legal decisions.

As a Forensic Psychiatrist, understanding the above core functions is essential for psychiatrists as courts increasingly request psychiatric input. Local legal systems may not always use the same terms as Western systems, but the underlying principles remain similar. By mastering these subspecialties, practitioners can provide accurate, ethical, and culturally informed evaluations.

1.4 Key Differences between General Psychiatry and Forensic Psychiatry

Although general psychiatry and forensic psychiatry share a common foundation in mental health assessment and diagnosis, the two disciplines differ significantly in purpose, ethics, methodology, and professional stance. General psychiatry focuses on the treatment and support of individuals experiencing mental illness, aiming to promote healing and recovery through a therapeutic alliance(Khosla et al., 2014). Forensic psychiatry, in contrast, is primarily concerned with providing objective, evidence-based evaluations that inform legal decisions. These distinctions shape every aspect of practice, from the nature of the psychiatrist–patient relationship to the standards of confidentiality and consent.

The main objective of general psychiatry is the provision of therapeutic care. Clinicians aim to help patients alleviate symptoms, perform better, and have long-term wellness. In general psychiatry, there is a long-term, cooperative manner, and decisions reflect positively on the patient(Khosla et al., 2014). Forensic psychiatry is more concerned with evaluation than treatment or cure. The function of the psychiatrist is to bring legal information, such as establishing the sanity of the accused at the time of the crime or capacity for medical decisions. Evaluation in such a field usually refers to a brief, focused assessment to solve specific legal issues, not to understand the mental status of an individual.

A significant difference can be seen in how the therapeutic relationship works in each field. Strong therapeutic relationships grounded on mutual empathy, trust, and teamwork represent the cornerstone of general psychiatry. The interaction in forensic psychiatry reflects detachment, untherapeutic, and sometimes confrontational. Candidates for forensic evaluations may not be interested in help and may feel anxious because of the procedure(Khosla et al., 2014). Those evaluated may try to deceive the evaluator, especially when the legal consequences could be grave. Forensic psychiatrists are professionally required to be objective and avoid creating a therapeutic relationship with the individual being assessed.

The standards of informed consent and confidentiality differ in these two areas. As a general rule, in psychiatry, one can only start treatment after receiving consent from a patient, and privacy is protected unless it is necessary to prevent harm. In forensic psychiatry, specialists must inform the subject that the evaluation is for legal purposes, that it is not confidential in the traditional sense, and that they will share the findings with the court or other requesting party(Franke et al., 2020). Explaining these boundaries at the outset is critical to maintaining ethical standards.

Objectivity is the most essential distinction. While general psychiatrists may advocate for their patients' well-being, forensic psychiatrists must remain impartial. Their duty is to the legal system, and they must base their opinions solely on clinical evidence and legal criteria, even if those opinions have negative consequences for the subject(Franke et al., 2020). It can lead to ethical discomfort, particularly for psychiatrists trained primarily in therapeutic roles. Forensic psychiatrists often face tensions between justice and care.

The above differences are important for psychiatrists expecting to give their opinions in court without experience in the field. Misunderstanding the role, pseudonymity, privacy, or dual relationships can result in legal and ethical dilemmas(Franke et al., 2020). Hence, there is a need for clear differentiation between general and forensic psychiatry to ensure patients are safe and receive the best services.

1.5 Ethical Considerations in Forensic Psychiatry

This work aims to establish that forensic psychiatry is a sub-specialty with its ethical issues distinct from general psychiatry. These challenges stem mainly from the fact that the psychiatrist is responsible for the legal process and the subject of the evaluation. Some ethical concerns that are likely to be faced include dual agency, informed consent, confidentiality, impartiality, and cultural sensitivity. Solving these issues presupposes a clear understanding of professional and legal standards, especially in countries where legal and religious systems influence the practice of psychiatry.

Dual agency happens when a psychiatrist tries to perform two functions simultaneously: a therapist and an assessor. This duality can lead to significant ethical dilemmas. For instance, a psychiatrist attending to a client may give an opinion in a legal case involving the same client. Such circumstances can be detrimental to the therapeutic alliance and result in prejudice (Glancy et al., 2021). Psychiatrists should avoid dual relationships as much as possible because they are unethical and interfere with the neutrality of the assessment.

Another critical ethical concern is informed consent. In clinical psychiatry, patients typically consent to treatment voluntarily and are informed about the nature of the therapy. However, in forensic psychiatry, courts or employers often mandate evaluations, and the individual being assessed may not have a choice. Despite this, it remains essential for experts to inform the person that the evaluation is for legal purposes, that no therapeutic relationship is being formed, and that they will share the results with third parties(Glancy et al., 2021). Transparency and respect for autonomy are fundamental ethical obligations, even in involuntary settings.

Confidentiality in forensic settings is limited. While general psychiatrists are bound to keep patient information private except in cases of imminent risk, forensic psychiatrists must disclose findings to the requesting authority. This disclosure includes sensitive details relevant to the legal question(Glancy et al., 2021). However, irrelevant information should not be included in reports out of respect for the individual's dignity. Psychiatrists must balance legal expectations with ethical discretion when reporting.

Objectivity and neutrality are the most crucial ethical standards in forensic psychiatry. The forensic psychiatrist must remain neutral, presenting findings based on evidence without favoring any party. It is especially challenging when working in adversarial legal systems, where opposing sides may try to influence the expert. The psychiatrist's primary obligation is to the truth, not to the defendant or the prosecution. Maintaining independence is vital for credibility and justice.

Another factor that may affect ethical practice globally is consideration of cultural and religious beliefs. It is important to be cautious and sensitive regarding family structure, honor, and gender roles (Glancy et al., 2021). For instance, a topic such as mental illness and legal responsibility may be framed differently based on a person's cultural background. However, forensic psychiatrists are to apply scientific principles while respecting cultural background and traditions, maintaining professional credibility throughout.

1.6 Relevance for Developing Countries' Psychiatry Trainees

The role of forensic psychiatry is gradually growing in developing countries. Nevertheless, a significant need remains to strengthen education and training programs in the field. In many developing nations, most forensic evaluations are conducted by general psychiatrists who often lack sufficient training in legal issues, professional ethics, and the preparation of reports that meet legal standards required by the courts. This gap poses a significant problem in providing standard and quality psychiatric assessments in legal settings. The psychiatry trainees must learn about forensic psychiatry's role and basic concepts, not only for professional competence but also for the justice system and patients' rights.

The first factor that has led to the enhancement of forensic psychiatry in developing countries is the complexity of cases that involve mentally ill people. Currently, the courts increasingly turn to the use of psychiatric expertise to determine criminal responsibility, the ability to stand trial, the risk of recidivism, and the mental condition of the parties involved in family or civil cases. Such cases are on the rise due to the rising awareness of mental health and the legal system that is slowly integrating the involvement of psychiatrists. However, the absence of well-developed forensic psychiatry programs in developing countries challenges psychiatrists to meet this demand competently and evenly.

Legal professionals and judiciary members' limited understanding of forensic psychiatry's value and role continues to marginalize the field while blocking its complete integration into the justice system. The gap between psychiatric evaluation interpretation under developing countries legal systems and Western legal standards emphasizes why trainees need preparation to understand these differences. Mental health professionals must use culturally sensitive practices where religion strongly influences legal systems and ethical decision-making processes.

Furthermore, the rules and regulations for writing forensic reports in developing countries should be standardized to resolve the trainee confusion regarding what information the court needs, how to present the psychiatric findings in a legally acceptable language, and how to deal with issues like malingering or consent. Inaccurate or unclear reports may cause misunderstandings, legal issues, or professional criticisms. Forensic training involves legal reporting, ethical reasoning, and knowledge of the DSM-5 (Diagnostic and Statistical Manual of Mental Disorders, 5th edition).

The correctional system also demands more psychiatrists with adequate forensic practice knowledge. Mental health issues are prevalent among inmates, and the psychiatrists serving in correctional facilities are in a dilemma of treatment and security. These trainees should be able to know how to treat patients while observing the set rules and regulations, as well as the safety measures.

Lastly, developing countries have a national opportunity to lead this field. These nations have produced a few forensic psychiatrists who have done their fellowships in Western countries. Their experiences show that forensic training is possible and valuable. Local programs in developing countries, seminars, and publications like this guide can fill the gap and enable the next generation of psychiatrists to practice competently in legal contexts.

Chapter Two: Legal System Basics for Psychiatrists

Understanding the legal system is fundamental for psychiatrists who engage in forensic practice. Forensic psychiatry exists at the intersection of psychiatry and law, which means that legal concepts, procedures, and structures shape much of what psychiatrists do in this field. The legal system defines the framework within which specialists conduct evaluations, sets the standards for evidence, and ultimately determines how the experts will use psychiatric findings(Wasser, 2017). An inaccurate understanding of legal procedures or expectations can result in poor evaluations, legal errors, or ethical problems. That is why forensic psychiatrists should be thoroughly knowledgeable about the functioning of courts, their rules, and how measures are employed, emphasizing the legal environment in which they work.

The combination of burgeoning legal frameworks and growing needs for mental health in developing countries has resulted in a higher demand for forensic psychiatric counsel. Courts, police, and other legal professionals frequently refer cases of mental illness to the assistance of mental health professionals to counsel in complex disputes. Judges, not necessarily trained in secular law, require psychiatric experts to express psychiatric symptoms in the appropriate terms for judges, a form of expression usually different than that learned in the general studies of law(Wasser, 2017). Therefore, forensic psychiatrists must possess skills in psychiatric assessment and a good understanding of the particular legal, regulatory, and administrative framework they work within.

This chapter outlines key topics for forensic psychiatrists operating in legal systems, such as an overview of criminal and civil law, different court systems, responsibilities of expert witnesses, and clinicians who provide treatment. Criminal and civil law represent two separate spheres of the legal system. As a result, the nature of questions that arise in each context differs; therefore, the suitable psychiatric evaluation is different. In a criminal trial, a psychiatrist could determine whether the defendants were conscious of their actions(Wasser, 2017). However, in a civil trial, the case may center on whether or not the individuals can conduct their day-to-day lives or care for their children.

It is essential to know about the organization of the court system. Different cases go to different courts, each with its own rules, expectations, and procedures. Depending on the nature of the case, psychiatrists interact with criminal, civil, family, juvenile, or administrative courts. Each context requires a tailored approach, and failure to adjust one's methods accordingly reduces the effectiveness and credibility of the evaluation.

Psychiatrists' roles also differ depending on whether they treat clinicians or expert witnesses. The treating psychiatrist works within a therapeutic framework and must prioritize the patient's well-being, while the forensic expert provides neutral, objective opinions to the court.

Confusing these roles leads to ethical violations and damages legal outcomes and therapeutic relationships.

2.1 Criminal and Civil Law: Core Differences

The two major legal systems categories are criminal and civil law. Each domain carries different goals, procedures, and implications for psychiatric evaluations. Forensic psychiatrists must understand these distinctions because their role in each domain varies significantly. Criminal law focuses on whether a person committed a public wrong and what consequences, such as punishment or treatment, are appropriate (Pejovic, 2001). Civil law focuses on private rights, responsibilities, and disputes between individuals or institutions.

Criminal law deals with offenses against the state or society. Examples include murder, theft, assault, and drug trafficking. In such cases, the government prosecutes the accused. Forensic psychiatrists assess two primary issues: whether the accused was legally sane at the time of the crime (criminal responsibility) and whether the accused is competent to stand trial (Pejovic, 2001). Criminal responsibility evaluates the defendant's mental state during the act. Did the person have a mental illness that impaired their ability to understand the wrongfulness of their actions?

On the other hand, competence to stand trial involves assessing the person's present mental state. Can they understand the charges, assist their lawyer, and follow courtroom procedures? These questions are essential for ensuring a fair trial and protecting the legal rights of the accused.

Civil law governs disputes between individuals or entities. In these cases, forensic psychiatrists often evaluate issues such as testamentary capacity (whether someone can make a valid will), guardianship (whether someone needs another person to make decisions on their behalf), and capacity to consent to medical treatment (Pejovic, 2001). These evaluations are usually more focused on current cognitive and emotional functioning. The psychiatrist must assess whether the person can understand information, appreciate consequences, and make reasoned choices. Civil evaluations are standard in cases involving older adults, individuals with intellectual disabilities, or people suffering from severe psychiatric conditions.

In different legal traditions, the issue of criminal liability is based on whether the person has the mental capacity and purpose to commit the act, which is why both cognitive and volitional components are essential. Criminal profiling usually focuses on the mental health of the individual at the time of the crime to establish whether the person understood the wrong they were committing and the consequences of their actions. Psychiatrists practicing in jurisdictions influenced by religious law must understand how theological principles shape interpretations of legal accountability. Mental illness is considered in moral, religious, and legal terms, making the psychiatrist's task more complex than in purely secular systems.

In Western jurisdictions like Canada and the United States, legal standards like the M'Naghten Rule or the Dusky Standard define insanity and trial competency, respectively. These rules focus on cognitive and functional impairments and are secular. Forensic psychiatrists trained in these systems must adapt when working in countries where legal and religious reasoning are often blended.

2.2 Structure of the Legal System

Forensic psychiatrists must be aware of the legal system in which they operate because their assessments must meet the requirements of the judicial system. Most legal systems worldwide have a hierarchy of courts, including trial, appellate, and superior courts. These systems also categorize courts by legal roles, including criminal, civil, family, juvenile, and administrative courts, each of which poses unique psychiatric and legal issues.

Criminal courts seek expert opinions of forensic psychiatrists to establish whether a mental illness influences the defendant's capacity to harbor a criminal purpose or to comprehend legal processes. In these cases, psychiatrists assess matters like competency and criminal responsibility. In civil and family law, there are issues of guardianship, capacity to consent, or parental fitness in custody cases where the opinion of a psychiatrist is sought (Steinert&Henking, 2022). In juvenile courts, the psychiatrist's tasks are to evaluate a young person's developmental age, psychiatric state, and ability to engage in the justice system.

Administrative courts deal with employment, public service, and regulations. These courts use psychiatric evaluations to determine competency to practice a profession, disability benefits, or the effects of administrative actions on the affected person's mental health. In these cases, psychiatrists need to directly correlate the clinical findings and functional abilities required by the legal matter (Steinert&Henking, 2022). Civil and criminal courts differ in the rules of evidence, the burden of proof, and the rules of procedure. Forensic psychiatrists should adapt their assessments to the legal requirements and demonstrate how assessment findings are relevant to the legal question. A lack of clear and specific information misleads the court and decreases an expert's authority.

In some countries where religion plays a significant role in the legal system, for example, in some countries of the Middle East, many judges study Islamic law rather than modern psychiatry or law. This context makes it even more important for forensic psychiatrists to present their findings in simple language that is culturally sensitive. Reports must be factual, understandable by non-professionals, and translated if needed (Steinert&Henking, 2022). Forensic professionals consider medical evidence and procedural requirements when making their evaluations. Knowing how different legal systems work helps mental health professionals provide more accurate and culturally appropriate assessments. In any country, forensic psychiatrists have to adapt to the court's structure, the nature of the legal issue, and the cultural values of the court system.

2.3 The Role of the Expert Witness

Being an expert witness is one of a psychiatrist's most important tasks in forensic psychiatry. An expert witness is not an ordinary onlooker but someone with specialized knowledge that helps the court make a decision. The expert witness translates psychiatric information, defines psychiatric conditions, and provides an opinion on how mental conditions influence behavior, cognition, or decision-making (Channaveerachari et al., 2022). This function has to be highly competent, non-biased, and unambiguous. As in many other jurisdictions, expert psychiatric evidence is now highly regarded in criminal and civil courts worldwide, but it must meet legal and cultural requirements.

The expert witness is quite different from the fact witness. A fact witness gives evidence based on what he or she saw or heard personally during the event. On the other hand, an expert witness gives opinions based on evidence, clinical findings, and professional opinion. The American Academy of Psychiatry and the Law (2015) has stated that expert witnesses should rely on facts, ensure that their opinions are scientifically valid and accurate, and disclose any limitations of their opinions. They must be qualified, neutral, and capable of presenting information comprehensibly.

In the legal system, the court, the Public Prosecution, or the defendant may request a psychiatrist to be an expert witness. In any case, the role of the psychiatrist is to the court and not the side that seeks the evaluation. This principle helps the psychiatrist be neutral and loyal to the truth rather than to the client(Channaveerachari et al., 2022). The expert witness should never take the side of the patient or legal party since this is against the code of ethics and dilutes the credibility of the testimony.

Serving as an expert witness requires understanding the cultural and linguistic context of the court. In many jurisdictions, judges receive legal training specific to their country's legal traditions and are unfamiliar with modern psychiatric terminology or clinical frameworks. Therefore, the psychiatrist must use simple, respectful language, avoiding unnecessary technical terms (Channaveerachari et al., 2022). For example, instead of describing symptoms solely using DSM-5 labels, the psychiatrist should explain how those symptoms affect behavior, responsibility, or intent in terms familiar to the court. A clear connection must be made between the psychiatric diagnosis and the legal issue under consideration, whether it is criminal responsibility, capacity, or risk of harm.

Another important aspect of expert witness work is communication during court proceedings. The psychiatrist must answer the judge's and lawyers' questions, clarify technical terms, and respond calmly under cross-examination. Being professional and composed under pressure is essential, as expert testimony often influences high-stakes legal decisions(Channaveerachari et al., 2022). In some countries, proceedings are usually conducted in the local language, so psychiatrists must ensure that written reports or verbal testimony are either given in the local language or translated accurately and professionally.

Ethically, expert witnesses must disclose if they are not qualified to answer a particular legal question. They should avoid overstating their conclusions and clearly outline the basis of their opinion. When psychiatrists maintain honesty about the limitations of their findings, they help the court make informed, fair decisions.

2.4 Treating Clinician vs. Forensic Expert

The distinction between the treating clinician and forensic expert is crucial in forensic psychiatry. Though both roles require psychiatric expertise, they serve different functions, and different ethical expectations govern them. Confusing the two results in ethical violations, compromised evaluations, and harm to the individuals involved (Hugaboom, 2013). For psychiatrists working in legal settings where formal training in forensic psychiatry is still emerging, clearly understanding this difference is essential for professional integrity and legal credibility.

A treating clinician delivers mental health care to support the patient's recovery. The therapeutic relationship depends on trust, confidentiality, empathy, and advocacy. The psychiatrists work closely with the patient, often over a long period, and beneficence (doing good) and non-maleficence (avoiding harm) guide them. The patient's well-being is the central concern, and decisions are made with the individual receiving care (Hugaboom, 2013). As such, treating clinicians avoid making certain judgments or disclosing sensitive information unless there is a direct benefit to the patient or a clear ethical justification, such as imminent risk of harm.

On the other hand, forensic experts play a non-therapeutic role. Their main task is to answer specific legal questions through psychiatric evaluation. These questions include: Was the accused mentally responsible at the time of the offense? Is the individual competent to manage finances? Does the parent have the mental capacity to care for the child? Forensic experts often evaluate those they are not treating, usually in response to a court request, and therapeutic goals do not guide the relationship (Hugaboom, 2013). Instead, forensic psychiatrists must be objective, honest, and neutral in reporting findings, whether or not they support the interests of those on assessment.

The dual role of clinician and forensic evaluator should be avoided whenever possible. A treating psychiatrist who is an expert witness may find it challenging to remain neutral, especially if they have developed a trusting therapeutic bond. Likewise, if patients learn that their treating psychiatrist is giving testimony that could harm their legal case, it may erode trust and damage the therapeutic relationship(Dahl, 2024). In forensic contexts, the justice principle often outweighs the beneficence principle. This shift in ethical orientation must be acknowledged and respected.

In practice, evaluations reflect the difference between these roles. Treating clinicians base their decisions on ongoing observations and informal conversations. In contrast, forensic experts use structured interviews, collateral sources (such as legal records, police reports, and witness statements), standardized psychiatric tests, and formal documentation(Dahl, 2024). Their assessments must answer legal questions in a format acceptable to the court and supported by clear reasoning.

The issue of confidentiality further highlights the contrast. Confidentiality is strictly protected in clinical settings and can only be breached under specific conditions (such as risk to self or others). In forensic settings, confidentiality is limited, and the specialists must inform the evaluated person from the beginning that they will share the findings with the court(Dahl, 2024). In some countries, where religious and legal expectations about privacy are strong, this requires careful and culturally appropriate explanation during the informed consent process.

Ethically, psychiatrists must be transparent about which role they are performing. Mixing roles without proper disclosure leads to mistrust, professional complaints, or legal challenges. Psychiatrists should document their role clearly in reports and communications and decline dual roles unless necessary and ethically defensible.

2.5 Summary and Takeaways

Forensic psychiatrists must operate at the intersection of mental health, law, and cultural values. The legal system is complex, involving criminal, civil, family, juvenile, and administrative courts, each with its own procedures, expectations, and ethical considerations. To respond, Knowing about legal norms and codes of behavior that distinguish psychiatric treatment from legal assessment is important for success in this position.

Criminal law differs from civil law in functions and objectives; hence, psychiatrists should be aware of this. The civil wrongs are of chief interest to the law, which relieves the state's burden and includes mental incompetence. The range of civil law covers interpersonal disagreements and discusses competency matters, particularly concerning the power to make health and financial decisions. The psychiatrist must carry out individualized assessments for each legal case, predicated on the court's standards and guidelines. Cultural or religious considerations like moral intent or spiritual responsibility are part of some legal systems of mental illness, and, therefore, cultural competence is a requirement for forensic psychiatrists more than clinical mathematics.

Knowing legal frameworks allows psychiatrists to put forward their expert opinions better and more precisely. Criminal, administrative, or family courts require the unique demands of each to be addressed in assessments and reports by psychiatrists. Knowing how the legal system is organized prepares mental health professionals to meet legal requirements better, especially in report formulation or the delivery of testimonies. Since, in some courts, religious laws are involved, the psychiatrists must adjust their statements in court to reflect the possibility of a lack of psychiatric comprehension by the legal staff.

One of the most important things is to understand the duties of an expert witness. Forensic psychiatrists are not even therapists; they provide unbiased, professional opinions that still aim to be helpful to the court. The duty requires an inclination to objectivity, neutrality, and the ability to succinctly and appropriately express psychiatric discoveries within the cultural context. Expert witnesses must disclose limitations in their assessments and avoid making conclusions that exceed their expertise. Courts rely on psychiatrists to present honest, fact-based findings relevant to the legal question.

A common ethical challenge arises when psychiatrists serve as both treating clinicians and forensic experts. These roles differ in purpose and ethical duties. While the clinician prioritizes the patient's welfare and confidentiality, the forensic expert serves the legal process and must maintain objectivity, even when the findings do not support the individual's legal position. Mixing these roles can create ethical conflicts and reduce the credibility of both the clinician and the evaluation. Psychiatrists should clearly define their role at the start of any case and avoid dual roles unless necessary and ethically justified.

Chapter Three: Criminal Responsibility and Insanity Defenses

Throughout the forensic psychiatrist's work, the determination of criminal responsibility is crucial because deciding whether a mental disorder affects a person's legal accountability for his behavior is part of his work. Courts presume that people deliberate and know what they are doing, but severe mental health problems can disturb judgment, awareness, or control impulses. In such cases, law systems allow the use of the defense of insanity, which recognizes certain mental illnesses that can nullify or mitigate the defendant's responsibility from the law(Farrukh&Samejo, 2024). This chapter describes the legal and psychiatric frameworks for determining criminal responsibility. It offers a glimpse of how forensic psychiatrists determine if a mental illness compromised a defendant's mental health during an offense.

The chapter also mentions the generally accepted rules of law for insanity, for example, the M'Naghten Rule, the Durham Rule, and the American Law Institute's Model Penal Code. Experts draw on these criteria when offering opinions on criminal responsibility to courts in the United States, Canada, and the United Kingdom. The chapter discusses how psychiatrists evaluate criminal responsibility, including obtaining background data, analyzing symptoms, and presenting findings to legal settings. The purpose is to ensure that trainees and professionals execute legal and fair evaluations that follow justice principles and clinical ethics.

3.1 Fitness to Stand Trial (FST)

FST refers to a defendant's capabilities regarding the understanding of legal processes and taking part in their defense during the trials. FST is evaluated by the defendant's ability to take part in court processes, not by their mental state at the time of the crime. The essence of FST is to assess the defendant's mental state to ensure that he or she can defend himself or herself appropriately and with sound judgment(Burgess, 2024). It is a significant aspect in the regions where the greatest emphasis is on maintaining due process and the right to a fair trial.

U.S., Canadian, and U.K. law require mental fitness to be determined before permitting a person to participate in the trial process. Fundamentally, FST assesses one's ability to be understood, communicate effectively, understand the law, and dictate ideas to a lawyer. It involves understanding the charges, who the players in the courtroom are, anticipating the risks of a conviction, and having the ability to cooperate on essential decisions like plea negotiations or testifying.

There must be a fitness evaluation whenever a doubt about a defendant's behavior, statements, or mental health background has been raised. Under conditions like schizophrenia, bipolar disorder, major depressive disorder, and intellectual disability, regular investigations into an accused person's fitness to stand trial take place. Delusions or hallucinations can affect an individual's perception of reality and intellectual disabilities, memory, concentration, or ability to reason(Burgess, 2024). Profound changes in emotion or anxiety can also undermine a person's ability to communicate well or make intelligent decisions.

Forensic psychiatrists establish the capacity of a defendant to represent himself in court using a structured interview, mental status exam, and data from legal and medical sources. In this regard, there is no focus on identifying the diagnosis but evaluating how the symptoms impact the defendant's ability to advance through the legal process. Psychiatrists are required to outline the way the mental health problems of a defendant influence his or her comprehension or cooperation with legal authorities(Burgess, 2024). In many instances, forensic psychiatrists appeal to such tools as the MacArthur Competence Assessment Tool-Criminal Adjudication (MacCAT-CA) to measure defendant cognition and ability to reason toward standing for trial.

Once there is a ruling that a defendant is unfit, the court proceedings are held abeyance until the defendant becomes fit to stand trial. For most defendants, the behavior involves psychiatric therapy and the provision of legal guidance, medication, and supportive treatment. In different areas, legislation has put a time limit on the detention of those in restorative treatment. In cases that fail to find recovery from treatment, other possible alternative legal measures may become the necessary steps.

Forensic psychiatrists are essential in ensuring the people on trial understand and participate fully in legal matters. These assessments ought to be unbiased, supported by reliable evidence, and have a detailed record to help judges make factual decisions on a defendant's state of mind. Keeping FST that honors legal requirements and the mental health needs of persons with mental illness ethically and compassionately.

3.2 Criminal Responsibility

Forensic psychiatry is primarily concerned with examining the concept of criminal responsibility. Criminal responsibility deals with the question of whether persons with mental illness should be held legally culpable for their criminal actions. Most legal systems have traditionally assumed that people act intentionally and with a clear understanding of what they are doing(Farrukh&Samejo, 2024). However, forensic psychiatry provides courts with a clinically validated system for deciding whether mental illness might have significantly impaired a person's ability to make rational decisions or exercise self-control at the time of the offense.

The law recognizes that severe mental illness can impair a person's understanding of their actions, moral judgment, or ability to control behavior. For these defendants, the concept of criminal responsibility is frequently controversial(Farrukh&Samejo, 2024). It is a common role of forensic psychiatrists to assess whether when a mental disorder occurred, it affected an individual's capacity to acquire the requisite *mensrea*. Their role is to provide specialized and factual expert testimony to help courts determine whether the defendant's mental disorder affected their capacity to be criminally responsible, not to resolve issues of culpability.

The process involves analyzing historical data to determine the defendant's mental condition during the offense. Psychiatrists review records from doctors, talk to people who have spoken to the defendant, review police documents, and compare witnesses' accounts. From this evidence, they determine whether the person's mental disorder was a critical factor in their understanding of the nature and consequences of their criminal act(Farrukh&Samejo, 2024). Their conclusions directly affect decisions like the verdict, sentencing, supervision of treatment, or placement in an institution.

From the start, court rulings have gradually strengthened and developed the link between law and psychiatry in criminal responsibility. Under most Western legal systems, specific guidelines define insanity, hence protecting the mentally ill from criminal liability. They give courts and experts a distinct model of dealing with rare but vital cases where an individual's mental health is a significant factor determining the person's accountability.

Professional proficiency in forensic psychiatric care demands a thorough understanding of such standards, particularly among the specialists in countries such as the U.S., U.K., and Canada, who study forensic psychiatry with the help of these standards for their legal systems. These standards, such as M'Naghten, Durham, and the ALI Model Penal Code, are as fundamental to current forensic psychiatric practice and are critical bounds of criminal responsibility.

3.3 Legal Standards of Insanity: M'Naghten, Durham, and ALI

Insanity criteria decide a person's mental capacity during criminal proceedings. The guidelines address the impact of mental illness on a defendant's intent to commit crimes and obedience to legal rules rather than simply an issue of the diagnosis of mental illnesses. Different standards represent opposite views of the amount of responsibility reduced under mental disorders.

Among the earliest and most commonly used standards of insanity is the M'Naghten Rule. British law, as it used to be in the 19th century, defines insanity through the M'Naghten rule as a legal case whereby the defendant cannot understand the nature or moral aspects of their actions due to a 'defect of reason from disease of the mind.' The fearless focus on cognitive awareness forces courts to consider whether the defendant was aware of the outcome of their action, legally and morally.

Daniel M'Naghten's case served as the foundation of the M'Naghten Rule, which states that a person who believes that a public figure is pursuing him can kill the latter. The court ruled that M'Naghten's delusions made him unable to understand the moral wrongness or the nature of his actions(Mario, 2024). This verdict has created the legal landscape for the insanity defense in the United Kingdom, Canada, and many U.S. states.

What makes the M'Naghten Rule valuable is its simplicity and ease of application in hearings. Judges have a readily available template for judging whether defendants know what they are doing. Limitations on its use are considerable. However, people who understand the consequences of their actions, due to psychiatric problems, are unable to control themselves and are not considered under the M'NaghtenRule(Mario, 2024). Under the M'Naghten standards, people may not be recognized as having an intentional limitation typical of what for instance seen in manic states, regardless of the degree of impairment.

When adopting elements of the Durham Rule, it was possible to eliminate such constraints concerning people. According to the Durham rule, the law would not criminally punish a defendant with unlawful behavior that a mental illness or defect directly caused. Clinical expertise was fundamental to this approach, giving psychiatrists greater leverage in determining whether or not a defendant could be held responsible. It defended the insanity defense by highlighting the numerous ways in which mental illness colors an individual's behavior.

The critics of the Durham Rule most noted its vagueness and use of expert psychiatric judgments. Since there were no precise regulations that could specify when mental illness was the last cause of an offense, this requirement mainly resulted in uncertain results in court cases. The sum of legal systems has abandoned the Durham standard over the previous several years due to the vague nature of its phrase and the confusion that surrounds its meaning. Its consequence: It has kept its role as a significant event in forensic psychiatry as it focuses on the varied influences of mental illness on human conduct.

The American Law Institute adopted the ALI Model Penal Code standard in 1962. The standard provides that the law can spare people criminal liability if a mental disease or defect precludes them from understanding the illegality of their actions or impairs their ability to act lawfully(Mario, 2024). Along with the two aspects of understanding the wrongdoing and the capability to adhere to the law, the ALI standard encourages a more refined and flexible approach.

Adding volitional impairment to the ALI framework implies the acknowledgment that individuals who are aware of their wrong deeds may lack the ability to control themselves because of mental illness. It enables forensic psychiatrists to identify and analyze the diseases that hamper a patient's ability to control impulses and executive skills. In addition, the standard provides for a partial impairment situation, in which mental disorders can leave a person with some understanding or control but not the full capacity to meet legal obligations.

U.S. jurisdictions adopted the ALI standard, but society criticized it after the Hinckley case, in which he was acquitted of charges because of insanity after his failed attempt to assassinate President Ronald Reagan. After public outcry, the authorities passed the Insanity Defense Reform Act of 1984, which limited the insanity defense in federal courts and did not consider the person's ability to control their actions. Several states responded by moving towards stricter rules on the defense of insanity.

Today, insanity defense laws vary from state to state, but they all tend to reflect the basic principles described in these frameworks. Several

U.S. states have kept adaptations of the ALI or M'Naghten criteria for insanity defense cases. The cognitive criteria established in the M'Naghten ruling are still the foundation in Canadian and UK jurisdictions, even though legal systems have adopted aspects of psychiatric expertise and individualized assessment.

Forensic psychiatrists need to know the legal standard in their jurisdiction and adjust their assessments to meet that standard. Their task is to decide whether the individual's mental illness, at the time of the offense, impaired their cognitive or volitional capacity to the extent required by law for insanity. Specialists provide detailed documentation, use coherent arguments, and make sure that they communicate their conclusions effectively to the court.

As a rule, the effectiveness of these standards in practice depends on the psychiatrist's ability to correlate clinical observations with legal criteria. Diagnosing a mental illness does not meet the legal requirements. The psychiatrist should demonstrate how the illness changed the person's grasp or conduct during the crime. This process depends on psychiatrists having a complete understanding of psychiatric disorders and legal lingo and the ability to explain how these things work together through systematic and transparent evaluations.

Forensic psychiatrists must work under strict legal standards when assessing criminal responsibility. Each of the M'Naghten, Durham, and ALI standards brings its perspective to understanding the role of mental illness in legal responsibility. Using their professional experience and skills, psychiatrists apply these standards to assist the legal system in correctly separating criminal actions from those who could be seeking to draw advantage from mental disorders. Psychiatrists, in their work, promote justice, maintain the safety of society, and offer needed care to those whose mental conditions protect them against full responsibility.

3.4 Case Examples of Insanity Defenses

Case studies illustrate how legal standards for insanity are applied and tested. Reviewing real or hypothetical cases helps psychiatrists understand how to assess criminal responsibility and present findings in a legally relevant manner.

Case 1: John Hinckley Jr. – Successful Insanity Defense (United States)

In 1981, John Hinckley Jr. attempted to assassinate U.S. President Ronald Reagan to impress actress Jodie Foster. At trial, Hinckley's defense presented extensive psychiatric evidence that he had severe psychosis, including delusional beliefs and obsessive behavior. He was diagnosed with schizophrenia and narcissistic personality disorder (United States v. Hinckley, 525 F. Supp. 1342 (D.D.C. 1981)). Forensic psychiatrists testified that Hinckley believed his actions were necessary to gain Foster's love. Under the ALI/Model Penal Code standard, the jury found him not guilty due to insanity because he lacked substantial capacity to appreciate wrongfulness or control behavior. Public outrage followed the verdict, and reforms, such as the Insanity Defense Reform Act of 1984, tightened federal courts' standards (Collins et al., 2020). This case continues to serve as an essential example of how a well-documented mental illness, clearly related to the offense, can be used to support a successful insanity defense when legal criteria are met.

Case 2: R v. Stone – Failed Insanity Defense (Canada)

In the Canadian case R v. Stone (1999), the defendant stabbed his wife 47 times and claimed to be in a dissociative state triggered by provocation. He argued that he experienced non-insane automatism, meaning his violent act occurred without conscious control but was not caused by a mental disorder. The defense proposed that Stone was temporarily overwhelmed and mentally shut down, leading to the killing without intent (McSherry, 2000). However, the Supreme Court of Canada rejected the defense. The court ruled that the evidence did not support the claim of automatism without an underlying mental illness. It emphasized that dissociation resulting from emotional stress did not qualify as insanity under Canadian law (Heilbrun, 2006). The ruling clarified that forensic evaluations must differentiate between pathological dissociation and temporary emotional loss of control. Psychiatrists must provide evidence linking a recognized mental disorder to criminal behavior and explain how it satisfies legal definitions of criminal non-responsibility.

3.5 Ethical and Cultural Considerations in Criminal Responsibility Evaluations

The issue of ethics and culture is critical in the determination of criminal responsibility in psychiatry. As experts in the courtroom, psychiatrists also have to deal with ethical issues and cultural practices of the society in which they operate. These responsibilities have different dimensions in some countries because they base legal interpretations on different/local statutory laws. Impartial action is the primary ethical responsibility of forensic psychiatrists. It is part of the psychiatrist's duty to act neutrally and provide the court with neutral and scientifically substantiated evaluations, not in the interests of the accused. Forensic psychiatrists must continue being independent to not succumb to social, personal, or professional pressures and compromise their support of the defense or prosecution. They focus on how their evaluation project is truthful and transparent. Such neutrality is necessary when assessing religious beliefs, national security, communitywide traumas, and situations that can cause significant social emotions.

One of the matters at stake is getting consent from the patients and protecting their privacy during forensic examinations. Although court-ordered evaluation is allowed by law, the assessment agents must inform the people that they need to know the aim and scope of the medicolegal assessment. If family honor and personal dignity are primary, revealing a mental illness can result in social stigma. In doing evaluations, psychiatrists should conduct their evaluations with compassion; inform the patients regarding the boundaries of confidentiality, and highlight that the evaluation outcome is for the court and not for therapy.

Cultural competence is equally vital. Some patients apply religious or spiritual language to characterize their symptoms. Terms like a feeling of possession during spiritual practices, visions, or religious guilt may be mistaken for psychiatric problems or maybe a cover for unrecognized psychosis or traumatic experiences. Psychiatrists should distinguish between cultural acceptance of certain beliefs and mental illness. Experts in religious issues or cultural psychiatry can help make more precise assessments.

The additional ethical issue is the potential for misrepresentation of roles. Medical professionals taking care of the patients should not take up a forensic position until and unless proper limits are determined. Clinicians engaged in treatment are supposed to act according to the ethical principles of care and advocacy, whereas forensic specialists should aim at legal accuracy and applicability. Both treating and forensic roles include the introduction of bias or ethical violations. Circling the restricted subspecialty opportunities in formal forensics, general psychiatrists have a specific duty to safeguard therapeutic relationships through legal evaluations.

In addition, reports must be easily understood and specific to the patient's culture. Judges and lawyers lack psychiatric training, so technical terms should be translated into practical, legally relevant conclusions. For example, rather than stating, "The defendant exhibits positive symptoms of schizophrenia," it is more helpful to explain, "The defendant was experiencing command hallucinations that impaired his ability to understand the wrongfulness of his actions." Ethical forensic practice requires clinical expertise, humility, transparency, and cultural fluency. In the context where law and psychiatry intersect, this balance ensures justice while safeguarding the dignity of those with mental illness

3.6 Summary and Takeaways

Criminal responsibility assessments are a legal, psychiatric, ethical, and cultural issue. In this context, the forensic psychiatrist's task is to assess whether a person's mental disorder affected their ability to possess the *mensrea* at the time of the crime. This chapter highlighted that one should know the legal demands, DSM-5, and cultural information to conduct valid and reliable forensic assessments.

Several legal frameworks across the world address insanity assessment. The M'Naghten Rule is a legal test that only considers the defendant's ability to distinguish right from wrong. Although more comprehensive, the Durham Rule has been less popular because of its ambiguity. The ALI/Model Penal Code standard, which incorporates both cognitive and volitional elements, provides a more nuanced approach and has been widely adopted in modified forms. New standards have led international laws to focus on changing the way mental illnesses are seen in the law.

Although self-standing, these standards align with current legal laws and ideas for enforcement. Anything that requires legal or moral proof should only be granted to individuals who show a consistent state of good mental health. Judicial systems call on this principle to exonerate those with mental illness, usually relying on psychiatric evidence of non-intent. Joint psychiatric reviews with locally adapted principles ensure that a way to justice is created respecting local values, particularly where these ideas are presented unpretentiously and respectfully.

While both are important to address, there is a difference in the scope of Criminal Responsibility compared with Fitness to Stand Trial (FST). Fitness to Stand Trial determines if a person prepares for court and checks mental health at the time a criminal action occurred. Judging an excursion to a trial includes formal deliberations, in-depth psychiatric evaluation, and evaluation of relevant areas of law. There is a prominent lack of uniformity standards for FST evaluations in jurisdictions where financial restraints or inadequate institutional traditions exist. An approach to filling gaps in standardized measurements is for forensic psychiatrists to develop appropriate and effective checklists and guidelines according to culture. Such initiatives cultivate objectivity, guarantee compliance with due process, and promote the generation of better, more accurate, and reliable legal findings well beyond the contested case.

Practical examples show why it can be hard to determine criminal responsibility. Severe mental illness, particularly psychosis,was the aspect that was critical in the Hinckley case to ensure the successful security of the insanity defense if psychosis was apparent. Conversely, the Stone case showed that judges doubt whether psychiatrist witnesses are in a position to provide unidentified, vague, or incomplete testimony. By identifying various examples, the chapter presents the notion that ethical and cultural considerations should be central to forensic practice. At evaluations, forensic psychiatrists must put aside their personal preferences, have a free disclosure of information to their patients, operate with professional objectivity, and “stand in” a balanced position, especially when the mechanisms of tension or real emotional explosion are in full frequency.

Chapter Four: Civil Competencies

Civil competencies concern legal and psychiatric skills that indicate whether people can make decisions regarding personal, financial, and medical affairs. The process of assessing civil competency in forensic psychiatry provides an opportunity to examine in detail how external factors can lead to mental illness, reduced intelligence, or constitutive impairments that impair judgment (Drogin& Barrett, 2012). Forensic psychiatrists are often called upon by courts to determine an individual's ability to give consent for medical treatment, write a will, manage finances, or need court-appointed guardianship. These evaluations have different purposes and should not be confused with criminal assessment. Responsibility (or fitness for trial) is the main issue in criminal evaluations, while in civil assessment, the main abilities connected with daily functioning and self-determination are evaluated(Drogin& Barrett, 2012). The aim is to ensure that vulnerable people are unharmed and, simultaneously, their fundamental rights uncompromised as much as possible. Due to an aging population and increased awareness of mental health issues, civil evaluations with forensic methods have increased. It will be necessary for psychiatrists to use clinically, legally, and culturally sensitive approaches during these assessments. The next chapter discusses the following four key areas of the topics under discussion. Permission to practice in the treatment, testamentary capacity, financial capacity, and guardianship. This subsection discusses consent, testamentary capacity, financial capacity, guardianship, and informed consent in high-risk populations.

4.1 Capacity to Consent to Treatment

In civil forensic psychiatry, the ability to consent to treatment is key. In other words, this process aims to test whether a person can understand, value, and use the proper judgment in choosing medical treatments. Despite the general assumption that individuals can make informed decisions, there are specific mental health issues that can compromise that ability and often require a formal evaluation to address those issues (Buchanan, 2004). Valid consent only exists where the person can understand the information, the implications, determine the tentative outcomes, and make an informed and voluntary decision. By complying with this standard, the patients preserve their autonomy and ensure that the help needed reaches those most vulnerable.

There are times when assessing the capacity to consent is a must. For instance, when schizophrenia patients refuse treatment, clinicians have to determine whether they have made a considered decision or delusions drive such. If this happens, older adults with dementia can agree to treatment, which they do not fully understand and are not aware of, or their procedures and the consequences thereof. For the decision to be both morally and legally sound, forensic psychiatrists use both clinical and legal standards to examine these cases(Buchanan, 2004). The experts should evaluate an individual's cognitive and psychological performance when making decisions instead of basing it only on their diagnosis.

Most jurisdictions use a four-part assessment procedure to determine a person's competency about treatment. Firstly, people should clearly understand their illness, the treatment offered, its benefits, risks, and other options. Secondly, they need to understand the link between the information given and their context. Thirdly, the individual should assess various treatment options regarding their outcomes and choose the best option. Finally, they need to be able to make and communicate a voluntary and consistent decision. The criteria help clinicians distinguish those who refuse treatment from those whose decision-making capacity is compromised.

Forensic psychiatrists typically conduct these evaluations through clinical interviews and use structured tools like the MacArthur Competence Assessment Tool for Treatment (MacCAT-T). This instrument assesses understanding, appreciation, reasoning, and expression of choice using standardized questions (Wang et al., 2017). For example, the evaluator might ask the person to explain their condition, what the proposed treatment aims to do, and why they have chosen to accept or reject it. The psychiatrist then compares the responses to legal criteria and documents the findings.

The law does not require perfect understanding or reasoning. Even people with limited education or unusual beliefs can still be competent if they can engage meaningfully with the information. What matters is that the decision depends on a rational process rather than a delusion, confusion, or coercion. Psychiatrists must be careful not to mistake disagreeable or unconventional decisions for incapacity(Buchanan, 2004). For example, refusing chemotherapy due to fear or religious beliefs does not mean a person lacks capacity, so long as they understand the implications and express their reasoning.

The concept of fluctuating capacity adds complexity to evaluations. Some individuals, such as those with bipolar disorder or delirium, are competent during periods of stability but impaired during episodes of illness. In such cases, it is essential to assess capacity at a time when the person is medically stable. If treatment decisions are urgent, surrogate decision-makers are involved, but the psychiatrist must document why the patient could not consent. Cultural context also plays a role. In some communities, patients rely heavily on family to make health decisions, and their apparent lack of independent reasoning reflects cultural norms rather than incapacity. Psychiatrists should approach such cases with cultural sensitivity, exploring whether the individual has the capacity but chooses to defer to trusted relatives(Buchanan, 2004). Evaluators should distinguish between voluntary delegation and actual inability.

Informed consent also requires voluntariness. Coercion, fear, or misunderstandings undermine the process. Power imbalances influence decisions in institutional settings, such as psychiatric hospitals or prisons. Forensic psychiatrists must ensure that individuals give consent freely and not as a result of pressure or misunderstanding. It includes explaining that the assessment is not for treatment, that the findings are reported to legal or medical authorities, and that an individual has the right to refuse participation. Clear documentation is crucial. Reports should address each capacity element, explain the reasoning behind the opinion, and describe how the findings were obtained. Well-written capacity reports support ethical decision-making and can be used in court or clinical settings to justify treatment decisions.

It should be noted that assessing a patient's ability to consent is not only the job of psychiatrists. Usually, the treating physician, such as the surgeon, internist, or gynecologist in charge of the patient's care checks if the sick person understands the proposed treatment. Psychiatric help is needed only if there is a worry that a mental disorder might affect the patient's ability to make good decisions. It shows that the clinician proposing a treatment must ensure the patient is fully informed and makes the decision freely.

4.2 Testamentary Capacity

Testamentary capacity is the legal and mental capabilities to make or amend a will. This area of civil competency is of great importance because it deals with the outlook over assets, recognition of relationships of family order, and the maintenance of autonomy of individuals after death. Referring to the established legal criterion of the 1870 case, Banks v. Goodfellow provides that for one to have testamentary capacity, then an individual must understand the nature of a will, the nature of the property one has, the number and identity of the potential heirs and not be deluded to the point of not making a decision (Aravind et al., 2024). This standard is still widely used in many legal systems worldwide, including law-influenced ones.

When an individual with suspected mental illness or cognitive limitation makes a will, most of the time, a forensic psychiatrist conducts a testamentary capacity assessment. Such appraisals generally take place after the death of the person in question. They are usually triggered because family members challenge the validity of the will on the grounds of the lack of capacity of the deceased. In some instances, psychiatrists must make a retrospective assessment through the pages of medical records, letters, witness testimony, and within the body of the will(Aravind et al., 2024). In fewer cases, a psychiatrist evaluates testamentary capacity during the person's life when lawyers or family members can foresee possible disputes.

Understanding the four components of Banks v. Goodfellow is critical for conducting a valid assessment. Firstly, the individuals must know they are making a will. It means understanding that the document directs how the specialists distribute their property after death. Secondly, they must have a general idea of the nature and value of their estate. It includes knowing about significant assets such as land, bank accounts, or valuable items. Thirdly, they must be aware of the people who might reasonably expect to benefit from the will, such as children, spouses, or dependents. This awareness includes both recognizing these individuals and considering their claims(Aravind et al., 2024). Lastly, the person must be free from delusions that directly affect decisions. For example, if someone believes without reason that their daughter is trying to poison them and disinherits her based on that belief, the will may be invalid.

Psychiatrists must not assume that a diagnosis of dementia, schizophrenia, or depression means the person lacks testamentary capacity. Mental illness affects decision-making, but the ability to make a will must be assessed directly. Even people with significant cognitive decline still understand simple concepts and make valid choices, particularly if the will is uncomplicated.

The evaluation process usually begins with a clinical interview. Psychiatrists explore the person's understanding of their estate, the reason behind the will, and their relationships with family members. They use open-ended questions to avoid leading the person to give desired answers. Structured tools such as the Testamentary Capacity Instrument (TCI) help organize the evaluation, though their use is less common than in treatment capacity assessments. The emphasis must remain on the person's reasoning, clarity, and ability to link their decisions to reality, not the decisions themselves. For instance, someone disinheriting a close relative must explain their reasons clearly without evidence of delusional thinking or coercion.

In retrospective evaluations, forensic psychiatrists face special challenges. The person is no longer available for direct assessment, so the psychiatrist must rely on documentation, medical records, witness statements, and sometimes recordings of the will-writing process. The psychiatrist's opinion must consider when the will was made and whether the person's mental condition at that time met the legal standard(Aravind et al., 2024). If the individual had a fluctuating condition such as bipolar disorder or delirium, the psychiatrist must evaluate whether the will was written during a lucid period.

Cultural and educational backgrounds also influence the evaluation. Some people lack formal education but still understand their property and family dynamics. In such cases, psychiatrists must avoid using complex tests or legal language that might unfairly disadvantage the person. Instead, they should use everyday language and assess whether the person can explain their decisions in their own words. Cultural competence is essential to avoid biased conclusions and recognize valid non-Western reasoning expressions.

Psychiatrists must document the evaluation thoroughly. The report should address the four Banks v. Goodfellow elements and describe the evidence supporting the conclusion (Purser, 2015). It should also explain the methods used, any tests administered, and the basis for judgment. If the psychiatrist finds that the person lacked capacity, they must explain how the mental impairment interfered with specific elements of the decision-making process.

These reports have serious consequences in legal proceedings. Courts rely heavily on psychiatric opinions to uphold or invalidate a will. Therefore, clarity, neutrality, and careful reasoning are vital. The psychiatrist is responsible for presenting findings in a language that would be understandable by legal professionals and avoiding, as far as possible, speculation or excessive clinical jargon.

4.3 Guardianship and Conservatorship Evaluations

Guardianship and conservatorship evaluations are the mentality to manage money safely, responsibly, and independently. It covers a spectrum of tasks, which include paying bills and budgeting, making investment decisions, and preventing financial exploitation. Forensic Psychiatrists usually find themselves called to assess this kind of civil capacity if there are fears regarding cognitive impairment, mental illness, or developmental retardation(Aravind et al., 2024). Financial incompetence is one of the first symptoms of dementia and also one of the primary vulnerability factors in the case of older adults. Correct assessments assist courts and families in determining whether an individual can go on managing his or her affairs or if the individual needs legal cover, such as guardianship or conservatorship.

Financial capacity is not an 'all or nothing' condition. It depends on the complexity of the task, the person's experience with finances, and the severity of one's impairment. For instance, a person with a mild case of memory issues will still be able to make regular payments but struggle with anything new, such as managing insurance policies or online banking(Aravind et al., 2024). A psychiatric evaluation aims to see if the person can understand financial information and reason and avoid substantial risks. The assessment should also conform to the autonomy of the person and avoid excessive restriction of their independence.

The evaluation process includes clinical interviews and functional assessment. Psychiatrists ask the individual to explain how they manage money, such as paying rent, budgeting for groceries, or creating a bank account. They also set real-life situations to evaluate judgment. For example, the psychiatrist might question what the person would do if someone phoned them suspiciously, asking for bank details, or if they noticed unusual charges on their account. Watching individuals think through these situations gives the psychiatrist an idea of their capacity.

Structured instruments like the Financial Capacity Instrument (FCI) or the Lichtenberg Financial Decision Rating Scale provide more elaborate assessments. They assess domains such as bill payment, financial judgment, and appreciation of financial concepts. Using structured tools increases reliability, particularly when legal settings may review the assessment.

In most cases, evaluations occur where family members or legal officers suspect financial exploitation. For example, older adults may suddenly make significant gifts to a new acquaintance, or persons with a history of mental illness may sign over property without a clear understanding. In such cases, the psychiatrist must determine whether the persons acted with full awareness or impaired reasoning, manipulation, or delusion influenced them. Importantly, the presence of unusual financial behavior does not prove incapacity(Aravind et al., 2024). The key issue is whether the person understood the consequences of their choices and acted voluntarily.

Cultural and social contexts must be considered. Financial decisions are shared or delegated in some families or cultures, especially among spouses or adult children. A person who has never written a check can still knowingly delegate responsibility. Forensic psychiatrists must assess whether there is a change from prior ability or a pattern of risky behavior that suggests loss of capacity. Also, the evaluators must be cautious not to mistake cultural norms for cognitive impairment.

Psychiatrists recommend guardianship when they find that a person lacks financial capacity. Guardianship is a legal arrangement in which authorities give another person the authority to make financial decisions on behalf of the individual. Courts require clear evidence before granting such authority, which limits personal freedom. Psychiatrists must explain not only the presence of mental illness or cognitive disorder but also how it interferes with financial functioning and creates significant risk.

Ethical practice requires the specialists to consider guardianship only when less restrictive options have failed. For instance, financial counseling, power of attorney arrangements, or supported decision-making provide adequate protection without removing autonomy. The psychiatrist's role is to assess capacity and advise on risks, not to make the best financial decision. The final decision lies with the court, but psychiatric input can be decisive in shaping the outcome.

Documentation is essential. Reports should include the referral question, background history, mental status findings, specific observations of financial reasoning, and a conclusion based on legal standards. Clear and structured reports improve credibility and help the court understand the basis of the opinion. Vague or overly clinical language weakens the impact and confuses legal decision-makers.

In legal proceedings, psychiatrists may testify. Their testimony should focus on the individual's reasoning process, awareness of consequences, and the consistency of their decisions with their past behavior. They should avoid expressing opinions about whether the person made a "wise" or "unwise" decision, as these are value judgments outside the scope of capacity assessment.

4.4 Informed Consent in High-Risk Populations

Informed consent is a foundational principle in medical and psychiatric practice, ensuring that individuals make voluntary decisions about their care with full awareness of the benefits, risks, and alternatives. However, the process becomes more complex in high-risk populations, those with cognitive impairment, severe mental can be negated by mental illnesses or disabilities or lack of choice for agreement (Amer, 2013). Forensic psychiatrists are critical in determining whether members of such groups can consent, mainly if serious consequences result from their treatment decisions. Consent should be informed and contain the following three important factors: capacity, voluntariness, and adequate information. Such a guarantee will be important as it helps protect the individual's freedom of choice against undue dangers.

Those in vulnerable circumstances often cannot consent because of the significant barriers. Such delusions that are typical of schizophrenia make it hard for patients suffering from it to understand the intricacies of treatment. Dementia patients commonly have difficulties remembering important information or understanding the medical advice presented to them(Amer, 2013). For severe acute distress associated with psychiatric emergencies, patients often find it challenging to understand and communicate their choices accurately. Coping with such complexities requires a thoughtful and orderly approach to evaluating decision-making capacity and communication.

The first responsibility of the psychiatrist is to decide if the person will meet the criteria to give consent. It involves informing the individual of essential facts, understanding the risks involved, reviewing available choices, and making a well-thought-out enduring choice. Wang et al. (2017) provide guidelines for using tools such as the MacArthur Competence Assessment Tool for Treatment (MacCAT-T) or the Aid to Capacity Evaluation (ACE) to support these evaluations. Comprehension, insight and the ability to make sound judgments are measured by structured tests administered through these instruments. Structured assessments assist in verifying consistent evaluation results by allowing psychiatrists to determine critical factors.

Some people can have stages of limited or changing capacity. A patient with bipolar disorder may not consent during a manic phase, but when they stabilize; their ability to make decisions may be restored. In such cases, the timing of capacity assessment should ideally be at the person's most lucid point. If consent is not immediately needed, it is both clinically and ethically justified to delay it until the patient is in a better, more stable condition. Conserving autonomy means recognizing and promoting capacity, regardless of limitations or changes.

The quality of language used and communication skills are essential for supporting high-risk groups. Problems with literacy and language proficiency can hinder an individual's understanding of communication. Numerous people get confused and frustrated by technical jargon or increased emotions(Amer, 2013). Forensic psychiatrists should adjust the process of consent to the individual's ability to understand. It involves using simple language, visual aids, repetition, or involving family members as supporters. Culturally appropriate communication improves understanding and reduces the risk of invalid consent.

Voluntariness is especially difficult to evaluate in institutional settings, such as psychiatric hospitals or correctional facilities. Individuals agree to treatment out of fear, pressure, or a desire for early release rather than true understanding. In such environments, psychiatrists must explore whether consent is genuine or influenced by perceived coercion. Coercion undermines the ethical foundation of informed consent, even if the information is accurate and the person appears to agree.

When capacity is lacking, substitute decision-making mechanisms are used. These mechanisms include legal guardians, healthcare proxies, or family members authorized by law. In some jurisdictions, emergency treatment is given without consent if the person is at risk of serious harm (Dalal, 2020). However, forensic psychiatrists must still document the individual's inability to consent and justify the use of surrogate decision-makers. This documentation should include specific observations about the person's reasoning, behavior, mental state, and efforts to explain the situation.

Research environments also have ethical consequences. Informed consent for clinical trials, especially those that involve reducing high-risk interventions such as experimental drug treatments and neuromodulation, requires strict safety measures to be satisfied. Hope or desperation, which obscures their risk assessment skills, drives some to do so. Psychiatrists must evaluate the person's ability and the appropriateness of engaging them in research(Dalal, 2020). Other precautions include seeking ethics committees, using independent advocates, and continuously monitoring consent.

Cultural variables greatly complicate the consent acquisition process in high-risk groups. In some communities, members depend on elders or senior figures to make decisions on medical treatment. In such settings, psychiatrists must distinguish cultural tolerance of decision-making from actual inability. Because of cultural norms and individual rights, making informed decisions calls for psychiatrists to do a deliberate and situation-appropriate review.

Forensic psychiatrists have an important but challenging task of obtaining informed consent from high-risk groups. Informed consent with high-risk populations is more than checklist completion; it is intentional patient observation, meaningful interaction, and situational assessment.

Psychiatrists meet legal and ethical requirements through organized procedures, clear descriptions of conditions, recognition of patients' partial capacity, and thorough documentation of evaluations(Dalal, 2020). With respect for rights and humane care, people are prepared to make responsible decisions in complex and urgent situations.

4.5 Fitness for Duty Evaluations

In civil forensic psychiatry, fitness for duty evaluations is crucial. These assessments aim to check if individuals have the mental and emotional skills to do their job safely and effectively. Most often, people in law enforcement, the military, aviation, emergency medicine, and healthcare are asked to take them. However, such issues can also occur in companies, universities, or factories if employees' actions suggest they might not be mentally stable or able to do their job.

Fitness for duty evaluations are not criminal or therapeutic but are usually requested by employers, licensing boards, or occupational health departments. These evaluations answer a specific question: Can the individuals do their job safely and without harming themselves, others, or the organization? This question often leads to important decisions such as returning to work, taking a leave, being assigned elsewhere, or being fired.

The initial part of a fitness-for-duty evaluation is to learn about the referral situation. Usually, a referral is made after someone shows erratic behavior, has emotional outbursts, makes threats, is absent often, or has performance issues. The referring party may think the individuals' mental health is interfering with their ability to do their job(Ferranti, 2017).

Sometimes, the referral is made after an injury at work, a violation of substance use rules, or a complaint by a whistleblower. The evaluator should determine the reason for the referral, identify the tasks being questioned, and check any relevant policies or regulations.

During a fitness for duty evaluation, a clinical interview, a review of employment records, and psychological testing are often used. The psychiatrist may also ask for reports from supervisors, co-workers, or staff in the occupational health department. It is essential to know the main tasks of the job; this is learned by reading job descriptions or talking to the employer. The evaluation should be targeted to the job and not a general mental health check; it looks at whether the people can handle their work's cognitive, emotional, and behavioral aspects.

Being objective is the main principle that directs these evaluations. The psychiatrist should not take sides or support the employee or the employer. In some cases, the employees may feel that the referral is unfair or harsh, especially if they do not know the reason for the evaluation. The psychiatrist should clarify why the assessment is being done, what information will be kept confidential, and how the findings will be delivered(Ferranti, 2017). Consent should be given, and the employee needs to understand that the results will be sent to the referring party in a summary report.

Being fit for duty does not depend only on whether someone has a psychiatric diagnosis. A person with a mental illness can still serve in the military if their condition is stable and controlled. If a person's behavior seriously affects workplace safety, decision-making, or relationships with colleagues, they may still be unfit for the job, even without a formal diagnosis. The psychiatrist should look at symptoms such as mood swings, poor judgment, or memory loss and decide if they affect the person's ability to do the job. Sometimes, the person may need to take a break for treatment and be assessed again before returning to work.

Ethics play a key role in these fitness-for-duty assessments. Dual agency is a frequent issue when the psychiatrist has previously worked with the employee in therapy. When this happens, the psychiatrist should not take on both roles. The person conducting the evaluation should not have any personal or professional connection to the individual(Ferranti, 2017). The review must be performed concerning confidentiality but within legal boundaries. The report should only contain details that answer the referral question; any personal or sensitive information that does not impact fitness should not be included.

The structure of reports should be clear, and they should be written to answer the referral question. A good fitness for duty report should summarize the background, explain the methods used, describe the person's behavior, include important clinical information, and state whether the person is fit for duty(VanDercar& Bruce, 2021). The conclusion should be clear: the patient is either fit for work, unfit for work, or fit with some conditions or requirements. The report may suggest that the company should occasionally reevaluate or consult with occupational health.

In certain areas, psychiatrists may be required to give expert testimony or speak before regulatory groups about their results. When this happens, the psychiatrists should be ready to explain their decisions with solid evidence and logical reasoning(VanDercar& Bruce, 2021). For legal and professional reasons, it is essential to record all the materials reviewed and the observations during the assessment.

Fitness for duty evaluations help link mental health with how someone performs at work. They depend on sound clinical judgment, knowing the job's requirements, and following all ethical and legal rules(VanDercar& Bruce, 2021). Forensic psychiatrists use facts and evidence to help ensure public safety and fairness at work.

4.6 Summary and Takeaways

Forensic psychiatry is heavily based on evaluating civil competencies when people cannot manage personal, financial, or legal affairs. In the area of forensic psychiatry, these competencies are discussed to protect people's rights and avoid any harm. The four major areas are the capacity to consent to treatment, testamentary capacity, financial decision-making, and consent of high-risk populations. Each one has its own legal standard and ethical requirements.

Consent ability for treatment includes understanding, appreciation, reasoning, and choice. Psychiatrists determine whether individuals understand medical info, can draw the importance of the info to their cases, and make decisions based on the information. Assessments are precise and respectful with the help of tools, such as the MacCAT-T or clear communication methods. Psychiatrists also have to look out for coercion, especially in institutional settings, and ensure that decisions reflect a person's free will.

Testamentary capacity requires that individuals understand the purpose of making a will, know the nature and extent of their property, identify the people who may have a rightful claim to their estate, and are not affected by a mental illness that could significantly impair their ability to make informed decisions. This capacity must be present at the time of making the will. Even people with cognitive disorders like dementia have testamentary capacity if the legal standard is met. Retrospective evaluations require careful review of medical records and behaviors near the time of writing the will. Psychiatrists must link mental symptoms clearly to legal standards in their reports.

Financial capacity involves making daily and complex money-related decisions. Psychiatrists assess if someone can budget, pay bills, avoid scams, and understand the consequences. Capacity loss increases the risk of exploitation and harm. The experts should consider guardianship only when no other support options work. Ethical evaluations must balance protection and respect for independence. Structured tools and functional examples help psychiatrists support their conclusions.

In high-risk populations, such as those with psychosis, developmental disabilities, or cognitive decline, informed consent becomes more difficult. Individuals face challenges in understanding or reasoning through medical decisions. Psychiatrists must simplify language, repeat key ideas, and test comprehension carefully. In settings like prisons or psychiatric hospitals, consent must be genuinely voluntary. Substitute decision-makers are needed when capacity is impaired. However, respect for partial or fluctuating capacity remains a key ethical concern.

Clear documentation is essential across all areas. Reports must describe the person's abilities, the methods used to test them, and the reasoning behind the conclusions. Psychiatrists must remain neutral; explain findings using non-technical language, and address specific legal standards. Clear reports and ethical evaluations help courts make decisions that respect individual rights and ensure safety.

Forensic psychiatrists must also consider cultural and social backgrounds. Different cultures express decision-making differently, and assumptions based on Western norms lead to incorrect conclusions. Psychiatrists should explore family roles, spiritual beliefs, and communication styles to understand the full context of a person's decisions.

Fitness-for-duty evaluations apply civil competencies to the workplace. Forensic psychiatrists ensure that mental illness does not put job safety or performance at risk for employers, employees, and the public. By using objective methods, documenting clearly, and being ethically neutral, administrative decisions are fair and support the discipline's primary goal of assessing function in modern workplaces.

Chapter Five: Risk Assessment and Violence Prediction

Violence risk assessment is one of the most essential duties in forensic psychiatry. It directly extends the preceding chapters on criminal and civil competencies by turning attention from the capacity to make decisions to assessing the potentiality for future malfeasance. Although forensic psychiatrists assist courts in determining a person's legal responsibility or capacity, they also respond to questions, such as, Is this person likely to cause injury to others again?" or "Is this person a danger to themselves or society?" These questions help to influence legal (judgment) decisions regarding detention, release, sentencing, and treatment planning.

In contrast to general psychiatry, where risk assessment involves time-limited, safety-focused clinical assessment, forensic psychiatry requires taking a bigger picture. Legal consequences, public safety, and long-term conduct should be considered during the evaluation. Structured violence risk assessments are more accurate and reliable than unstructured clinical judgment alone. Such resources enable psychiatrists to organize relevant data, neutralize existing biases, and report risk assessments clearly to the courts and relevant institutions.

The subsequent pages demonstrate how acute care psychiatrists use standardized tools and their expert knowledge to assess various types of risk. Firstly, addressing general violence risk measures and then moving on to instruments for those with suicide risk in forensic populations. It then goes on to look at some of the significant examples of targeted risk: stalking, domestic violence, and violence at work. The chapter also delves into ethical principles, detailed documentation processes, and culturally sensitive approaches that are ideal for all the aspects presented. This chapter's objective is to provide psychiatrists with an accessible yardstick for risk quantification whenever clinical and legal issues coincide.

5.1 Structured Tools for Evaluating Violence Risk

Risk assessment plays a critical role in good scientific decision-making in forensic psychiatry. Clinicians determine whether or not there is a danger that a person will harm himself or others. These assessments are the foundation for deciding whether a person deserves admission to a hospital, release from detention, receive a sentence, or be placed under supervision(Ogonah et al., 2023). Since forensic psychiatry is in a unique area between medicine and law, the knowledge required must be detailed, standardized, and organized. When clinical judgments are not standardized, the results can be inconsistent and unreliable.

The HCR-20 (Historical, Clinical, Risk Management-20) is essential for making professional judgments in forensic psychiatry. The assessment platform consists of three parts and has 20 items: historical elements, clinical elements, and risk management. By using HCR-20, clinicians can score every item and merge the scores to get a broad risk profile instead of a single one(Ogonah et al., 2023). This approach allows clinicians to consider all the details of the case before deciding, unlike when they use only a single piece of information.

The Violence Risk Appraisal Guide (VRAG) is another widely recognized assessment used in correctional settings. In Canada, the VRAG was developed using 12 critical factors found in statistics about violent recidivism, including age at the first offense, scores on psychopathy scales, and past felony history. HCR-20 uses a precise definition, while VRAG assigns scores to different risks. According to Helmus and Quinsey (2020), the VRAG is very good at predicting violent re-offending in men who have antisocial traits and a criminal background.

Both tools offer advantages. The HCR-20 supports subtler clinical judgment, particularly when used by competent professionals aware of the individual's context. The VRAG is less subjective and easier to reproduce, so it appeals to legal decision-makers who like quantifiable results. However, each has limitations(Ogonah et al., 2023). The VRAG is not helpful for women, adolescents, or non-criminal persons. The HCR-20 is subjective and can be biased if not measured well. The best practices include tools, up-to-date information, and clinical observations with empirical data.

Forensic psychiatrists should appreciate that risk assessment is not a one-off business. It is a repetitive exercise that increases with the individual's changing conditions. For instance, a person found to be low-risk during the arrest can develop acute psychosis or suffer destabilizing events in life, which increase the risk. The structured tools support this view by featuring dynamic elements such as present symptoms, social supports, and therapeutic compliance.

Any written documentation of risk assessment findings must be clear, organized, and tied to observable behaviors. Reports should describe the tool used, each item's supporting evidence, and how findings impact the conclusion. For instance, a psychiatrist may report that a client has a long history of impulsive violence, currently manifests paranoid delusions, and does not have stable housing, all factors that predispose to future aggression.

Ethically, psychiatrists must be open and honest about the limits of prediction. No tool guarantees certainty. Instead, they present probabilistic and risk information as evidence. Professionals should communicate these limitations to the courts and institutions while avoiding language that seems to lead to deterministic conclusions. Saying that a person "will re-offend" goes beyond the evidence. In contrast, by claiming that it is someone's "moderate to high risk," an individual realizes the uncertainty and facilitates planning for risk management.

Cultural competence also contributes to risk assessment. Trauma, discrimination, and mistrust of institutions influence behavior in a way that looks like risk markers but has a different meaning. For instance, the defensive behavior of someone from a high-violence community may not necessarily mean that such a person wants to attack others, but rather is a self-defense act. Psychiatrists should learn to analyze behaviors during contextual circumstances and not make too much of culture-driven responses(Ogonah et al., 2023). This calls for training, reflective practice, and interaction with the person's history and surroundings.

Credible tools such as HCR-20 and VRAG make violence risk assessments more precise and valuable in forensic psychiatry. They give a common reference point for combining historical, clinical, and contextual dimensions that help improve decision-making in legal and clinical contexts. Nevertheless, these tools should be used with care, ethical sensitivity, and an awareness of their limitations. Psychiatrists who use structured means and explain findings precisely contribute to justice, safety, and human treatment.

5.2 Suicide Risk in Forensic Populations

Suicide risk assessment is arguably one of the most important jobs of a forensic psychiatrist. The criminal justice system exposes individuals to higher suicide risk than the mean population levels because of incarceration, legal pressures, psychosocial stress, mental health problems, substance use, and previous trauma experiences. Suicide is the leading cause of death among prison populations, and the risk is much greater when compared to the community (Fazel et al., 2017). For that reason, forensic psychiatrists need to assess suicide risks carefully, document outcomes precisely, and participate in developing a plan that minimizes the risk of self-harm in places like jails, hospitals, and courts.

Suicide risk is not static. It changes depending on mental state, surroundings, and access to means. Forensic populations differ since isolation, shame, guilt, and lack of future certainty exist. For instance, awaiting trial persons might experience a serious psychological downfall in cases where the courts charge them with grave offenses or the fear of long sentences(Kaggwa et al., 2023). The first stage of incarceration is a high suicide risk period, especially for those who have not yet adapted to the new environment and may feel powerless or overwhelmed.

In the first stage, the identification of well-documented risk factors for suicide is an essential factor in the process of assessment. The established risk factors include a previous attempt at suicide, major depressive episodes, psychosis, alcohol or drug use, impulsive behavior, and recent challenging life situations. The risks associated with the forensic context, including loss of freedom, appearing in public with humiliating behavior, and being separated from family, significantly increase the level of danger(Kaggwa et al., 2023). Providers should obtain comprehensive data on suicidal thoughts, intent, and opportunities for suicide, as well as factors preventing suicidal actions. The omission of such discussions can make one presume that the patients will be less of a safety problem than they are.

Structured instruments are an essential part of how forensic psychiatrists undertake this task. The use of the Columbia-Suicide Severity Rating Scale (C-SSRS) as a set tool for the assessment of suicidal thoughts and behaviors is, in most cases, recognized. The psychiatrists use the scale to ask respondents about thoughts of death, specific intent, steps taken to plan, and their past actions concerning suicide(Kaggwa et al., 2023). This framework, referred to as SAFE-T, helps evaluators to determine possible risk and protective factors and make informed judgments about the severity of the patient's risk. Using these instruments, clinicians can record their assessments systematically and maintain consistent reporting.

Although these instruments are helpful, they are not a complete solution. A thorough suicide risk assessment should include careful observation, review of information from various sources, and consideration of the person's circumstances. For example, a person may say that they do not have suicidal thoughts, but they show withdrawal, hopelessness, or psychosis, which means that the risk is still present. Discussion with family, consultation of medical histories, and involvement of custodial staff can reveal important aspects of a person's situation(Kaggwa et al., 2023). Clinicians sometimes prefer checklists to judgment, which can undermine the effectiveness of the assessment.

The cooperation of individuals outside the clinical team is key to forensic suicide prevention efforts. Besides recognizing early warning signs, judges, correctional officers, probation officers, and social workers should be informed to report such. On many occasions, forensic psychiatrists are often the people responsible for coordinating and heading the efforts of institutions in the prevention of suicide(Guo et al., 2021). Programs may include increasing vigilance, protecting the environment against lethal instruments, permanent psychological aid, peer support, and adaptation to surroundings. Systems aimed at creating early identification as well as facilitating collaborations for staffs significantly reduce the rates of suicides in correction facilities.

From the ethical point of view, the execution of the suicide risk assessment is a complicated balance between two things: the protection of a person and the protection of the rights of a person. Self-harm is prevented through involuntary hospitalization or isolation, although this causes distress or negates personal autonomy. Psychiatrists must base decisions on current mental state, risk of harm, and the least restrictive option available (Guo et al., 2021). They must also explain to the individual the reasons for any safety measures, even if those measures are temporary or unpleasant. Clear communication reduces confusion and resentment and helps maintain therapeutic rapport.

Documentation is essential. Reports should include the person's statements, behaviors observed, pertinent history, risk and protective factors determined, and the final evaluation by the psychiatrist. Documentation should also include risk management plans such as close supervision, hospitalization, or referral to mental health professionals. The absence of documentation in risk assessments frequently leads to suing psychiatrists, receiving complaints from authorities, or losing the opportunity to protect patients (Guo et al., 2021). Clear and detailed documentation is a reliable benchmark for continuous evaluations.

Different cultures express emotional pain in various ways. Suicidal intent can be indicated in terms of a person's religious beliefs, but also through behavior, which are private or gentle. The ability to correctly understand meaning and intention requires that psychiatrists take into consideration concepts of cultural expressions of death, language conventions, and attitudes within the community toward mental health. Knowledge of the forms of cultures greatly enhances the accuracy and value of suicide risk evaluations within patients.

Forensic patients should be provided with a systematized and flexible mechanism for evaluating their risk of committing suicide. When assessing forensic patients, forensic psychiatrists should consider manifestations of warning signs, use scientifically proven tests, search for additional evidence, and use their specialist skills (Guo et al., 2021). They should base practical work on ethical practice, respect cultural differences and describe observations accurately. The action can support the process. Such practices enable psychiatrists to act and prevent further damage and save people who are under legal threat.

5.3 Stalking, Domestic Violence, and Workplace Threats

There is a growing need on the part of forensic psychiatry to evaluate cases of stalking, domestic violence, and threats at work. The process of carrying out evaluations involves moving through difficult social and emotional environment and is risky to safety. The majority of the targeted violence in such settings is associated with obsessive or justice-oriented feelings rather than spontaneous behavior or intent to commit a crime. The management of such forms of violence necessitates that forensic psychiatrists should examine the interpersonal relationships that are causing the aggressive behavior carefully.

In a professional setting, stalking is defined as the constant pursuit of a person, even if they are anxious or in real danger because of it. Targeted individuals can be stalked in real life, on the internet, or through constant messaging from the stalker. Stalking risk evaluation by forensic psychiatrists entails examining the relationship dynamics between the stalker and target, the obsessive or delusional tendencies, and the stalker's background. Stalkers exist in subtypes: the rejected (after a breakup), the intimacy seekers (who want an undisclosed relationship), or the resentment stalkers (who want retaliation). Each subtype entails different risks; managing each subtype usually requires customized approaches.

Tools like the Stalking Assessment and Management (SAM) guide clinicians through key areas, including the intensity of pursuit, threat credibility, and environmental support. Psychiatrists must assess the risk to the target and the likelihood of continued behavior despite legal interventions. For example, a person with erotomanic delusions may believe the target reciprocates their affection and may not respond to restraining orders. In such cases, treatment of the underlying delusion is essential. Interventions that combine legal restraint with psychiatric care are most effective.

Domestic violence (also known as intimate partner violence (IPV)) refers to physical/ emotional/ sexual/ or financial abuse in a close relationship. Risk assessment entails detecting patterns of control, escalation, and lethality. Attempts to suffocate the partner, threats with weapons, extreme jealousy, and separation are among the main predictors of lethal violence. The Danger Assessment (DA) is a validated instrument to identify risk cases regarding such factors.

The person providing the assessment of IPV has to assess the perpetrator's mental status and the relationship dynamics. There is a risk of violence associated with substance use, impulse control, antisocial personality traits, and past trauma. Meanwhile, they have to think about the victim's point of view, which can be careless about the danger because of fear, being dependent, or hoping for reconciliation. Victims tend to come back to their abusive partners repeatedly before they get themselves out permanently, and risk assessment must reflect this cycle.

Cultural and gender norms also determine how domestic violence is viewed and reported. In some cases, in some communities, victims might be stigmatized or retaliated against when they are reported, while in other cases, the perpetrators can justify their actions through cultural beliefs. A forensic psychiatrist must recognize how feelings of shame, the importance of honor, and their responsibilities can influence someone's willingness to open up. Such influences benefit assessments and interventions by adding cultural factors but never encourage negative actions.

Workplace threats refer to people who might be violent in the workplace. Such circumstances occur if an employee acts in a threatening manner, is emotionally unstable, or focuses too much on a manager or coworker. On occasion, a former employee, a client, or anyone outside the organization is a threat. Some warning signs are sudden behavior shifts, staying focused on issues of unfairness, making open threats, and pulling away from social life.

The Workplace Assessment of Violence Risk (WAVR-21) is a tool specially developed for evaluating people who might be threat actors in a work environment. It examines personality traits, the kinds of stress at work, aspects of the organization, and how people behave. Forensic psychiatrists collaborate with employers, legal experts, and police to design plans that monitor employees, steer them toward counseling, or adjust various workplace features.

In many cases, workplace violence is planned and developed as a result of grievances. People who plan workplace attacks usually hint at it with writings, spoken threats, or actions that are different from usual. Therefore, psychiatrists look at the patient's level of preparation, access to weapons, and enthusiasm to attack, typically without hearing threats directly.

It is essential to take early action when dealing with stalking, domestic violence, and threats at work. Once someone has been harmed, the negative impacts may never be fixed. Forensic psychiatrists contribute by identifying warning signs, documenting findings, and communicating risks to legal and organizational stakeholders. Their evaluations must be practical, forward-looking, and linked to concrete management strategies.

Ethical issues arise when psychiatrists balance confidentiality with the duty to warn or protect. If an individual reveals intent to harm a partner or coworker, psychiatrists are required to breach confidentiality and notify potential victims or authorities. Such decisions must depend on clear and immediate risk, supported by clinical evidence, and documented thoroughly.

The risk assessment targeted at perpetrators of stalking, domestic violence, and workplace harassment should focus on relational behaviors, intentions, and indicators preceding harmful actions. Professional knowledge of forensic psychiatry will be necessary for recognizing threats to safety and intervention efforts and protecting persons who can potentially be victims. Combining a reliable tool, professional judgment, and cooperation between disciplines will make risk assessment valid and applicable.

5.4 Summary and Takeaways

In forensic psychiatry, it is most important to determine the probability of violence. It directly impacts significant safety, treatment, and legal decisions. Psychiatrists assess whether individuals present a threat to themselves or others in different settings: prisons, hospitals, courts, homes, and workplaces. Such evaluations will need structured, evidence-based procedures to combine them with clinical judgment, ethical sensitivity, and cultural sensitivity.

Tools like the HCR-20 and VRAG have changed how forensic psychiatrists address violence risks. These tools help organize information, guide judgment, and restructure the reentry of information from cases into a comprehensible form (using historical data, clinical observations, and environmental factors). The HCR-20 promotes narrative formulation and flexibility, whilst the VRAG delivers relative statistical risk categories. Such instruments enhance the reliability and transparency of predictions of risk, in particular, when applied in the hands of trained clinicians. Even so, psychiatrists should avoid overreliance on scores and always interpret findings in context.

Suicide risk is a significant concern in forensic settings. Incarcerated people, people with serious charges, and people who have co-occurring mental illness and substance use are at increased risk. Past periods of detention, recent losses, or psychiatric symptoms that are still untreated can be predisposing agents for suicide attempts. Psychiatrists use the C-SSRS and SAFE-T as structuring tools, although they also need to observe, interview, and source collateral information. They cooperate with custodial and clinical staff to create and incorporate risk management plans, including hospitalization, monitoring, and therapeutic actions. Ethical decision-making is essential, especially when making adjustments related to balanced autonomy and protection.

Stalking, domestic abuse, and workplace threats are forms of targeted violence that have unique assessment strategies. Such behaviors are usually rooted in personal resentment, obsession, or control tendencies. Such resources as the Stalking Assessment and Management (SAM), Danger Assessment (DA), and WAVR-21 are helpful tips for identifying candidates for escalating behavior toward harmful actions. Psychiatric evaluations involve concerns about motivation, examining mental illness or delusional thinking, and searching for behavioral warning signs. Collaboration with law enforcement, courts, and employers on a multidisciplinary level is necessary for successful prevention.

Across all types of risk, forensic psychiatrists must address several key principles.

Risk is dynamic. It changes with context, time, and clinical state. Experts should conduct reassessments regularly.

Tools support but do not replace judgment. Structured instruments guide thinking, but the psychiatrist's insight and context-specific reasoning remain essential.

Documentation is critical. Reports must link observations to conclusions, use accessible language, and explain the rationale behind recommendations.

Ethical concerns are constant. Specialists must address confidentiality, consent, and cultural respect in every evaluation.

Cultural and systemic awareness improves fairness. Evaluators must avoid bias, understand systemic inequalities, and interpret behaviors within relevant social and cultural frameworks.

Forensic psychiatrists assess and facilitate risk management, resulting in usable plans that defend people and the public. When advocating for psychiatric care, informing legal decisions, or influencing institutional policy, their role does not stop with diagnosis; it also reaches prevention and public safety levels. As the field grows, psychiatrists must be up-to-date with research, hone their abilities, and continue their education.

This chapter follows previous commentary about criminal and civil competencies, illustrating their application to predictions of harm (assessment of capacity, intent, and judgment). Whereas previous chapters answered questions regarding the legal definitions of responsibility and decision-making, this chapter demonstrates how psychiatrists use that knowledge to answer future-oriented questions: Who might act violently? Who is bound to relapse into self-inflicted self-harm and aggression? Moreover, how can professionals intervene early?

Through expertise in these dimensions of forensic evaluation, psychiatrists live up to their responsibility to contribute to justice and to provide safety for mentally ill individuals in complicated legal systems. Predicting violence may never be scientifically perfect, but a structured, ethical, well-informed approach will make decisions as fair, open, and protective as possible.

Chapter Six: Psychiatry in Corrections

Correctional psychiatry is a vital part of forensic mental health. As incarceration rates rise globally, prisons and jails have become one of the largest settings for the care of individuals with serious mental illness. Individuals with conditions like schizophrenia, bipolar disorder, and major depression are over-represented in correctional facilities, often due to systemic failures in community mental health care(Fovet et al., 2024). Once inside, they face conditions that worsen their symptoms and make treatment difficult.

This chapter explores the role of psychiatry within correctional systems. Forensic psychiatrists working in these settings must provide care under conditions that are often hostile to therapeutic practice. The chapter begins with an overview of the challenges of delivering mental health care in jails and prisons, where limited resources, stigma, and security concerns complicate treatment. It then discusses solitary confinement, the use of restraints, and the ethical dilemmas psychiatrists face when human rights are in question. Lastly, it examines the difficulties of prescribing and managing psychiatric medication in incarcerated individuals, particularly those who resist treatment or misuse medication.

6.1 Mental Health Care in Jails and Prisons

The correctional system houses a disproportionately high number of individuals with mental illness. According to Fazel and Baillargeon

(2011), people with psychiatric disorders are three to six times more likely to be incarcerated than those without such conditions. Many arrive in custody already diagnosed, untreated, or undertreated. Others develop psychiatric symptoms in response to incarceration-related stress. Forensic psychiatrists play a key role in addressing these challenges, ensuring that incarcerated individuals receive ethical and practical mental health care.

Mental health care in correctional settings differs sharply from hospitals or outpatient clinics. Authorities primarily design jails and prisons for custody, not treatment. Security procedures, limited staffing, poor infrastructure, and high turnover create significant barriers to care. Mental health services in many facilities are underfunded and reactive, addressing crises rather than offering continuous care. Psychiatrists often work in isolation, with limited access to case managers, psychiatrists, or social workers.

Initial screening at intake is crucial. When individuals enter custody, they do not disclose psychiatric symptoms due to fear, stigma, or distrust. Standardized intake screening tools, such as the Brief Jail Mental Health Screen (BJMHS), help identify at-risk people(Testoni et al., 2021). Forensic psychiatrists then conduct formal assessments, reviewing history, medications, and current functioning. Early identification allows timely intervention, reducing the likelihood of suicide, aggression, or deterioration.

In correctional settings, psychiatric diagnoses often include psychotic disorders, major depression, bipolar disorder, and post-traumatic stress disorder (PTSD). Substance use disorders are also common and frequently co-occur with other conditions. These dual diagnoses complicate treatment, particularly when withdrawal or intoxication mimics psychiatric symptoms. According to James and Glaze (2006), more than half of incarcerated individuals with mental illness also have a substance use disorder, and most do not receive adequate treatment.

Access to therapy is limited. While some prisons offer cognitive-behavioral therapy (CBT) or group sessions, many facilities cannot support consistent, evidence-based psychological interventions. In jails, which often hold inmates for short periods, treatment is even more difficult. Medication becomes the primary tool for managing symptoms, but without complementary psychosocial support, outcomes are limited.

Crisis response is another core function of correctional mental health care. Inmates experiencing acute psychosis, suicidality, or severe depression require emergency intervention, including segregation, observation, or transfer to psychiatric units. Forensic psychiatrists must balance the need for safety with the risks of isolation or overmedication. Segregation is, at times, used as a substitute for mental health care in correction facilities when resources are limited. It should be possible for clinical psychiatrists to condemn such measures and advocate for compassionate measures of care.

Continuity of care continues to be an enduring challenge. Inmates often go to jail with prescriptions for psychiatric drugs but are usually required to surrender them or become unavailable upon arrival to custody.

Some prisoners start therapy while in prison but lose access to it when released from prison. Forensic psychiatrists have to coordinate intensely with community services to ensure that a patient does not relapse, overdose, or end up on the streets after being released(Testoni et al., 2021). Discharge planning is an essential component of moral behavior in cases of severe mental illness or a high level of risk of reoffending.

The stigma factor, which is real in correctional settings, hurts patients and medical personnel accessing or providing care. Countless inmates do not go for mental health care because they are concerned that they may be stigmatized or punished. Correctional staff often perceive the manifestation of mental health problems as weakness or intentional behavior, and consequently, there is little support and comprehension. Psychiatrists should educate employees, develop patient trust, and change beliefs that prevent services. Instilling teamwork between various experts whilst embracing learning continuously improves the quality of life for workers and inmates.

The role of a caregiver and a member of a security-oriented correctional team presents a set of complex ethical issues for forensic psychiatrists. Proper protection and confidentiality are essential, but patient safety is a top priority. Success means effective transparency, informed permission when feasible, and clear restrictions. For example, psychiatrists have a duty towards their patients to tell them the rationale for the security assessment they make and the possible consequences of it.

A clear understanding of roles eliminates ethical dilemmas and allows responsible practice.

Innovative programs show promise. Some systems have established mental health courts, diversion programs, and reentry planning groups to reduce recidivism rates and achieve the best outcomes. Proficient staffs in in-prison psychiatric services attend to the seriously ill, help stabilize them, and connect them with community mental health resources. Telepsychiatry has increased the accessibility of care in rural or inadequately staffed settings(Testoni et al., 2021). This evidence emphasizes that sound investment and strategic planning allow successful correctional psychiatry.

There are considerable barriers to dealing with mental health in correctional facilities, such as inadequate budget, stigma, and ethical dilemmas. Nevertheless, forensic psychiatrists are essential in advocating early screening, providing proper treatment, consulting with crises, preparing patients for release, and staff education. They advocate for a humanizing system where patients are lamely incarcerated and not cured. Clinical excellence and adherence to ethical guidelines help some of the riskiest strata in society benefit more.

6.2 Solitary Confinement, Restraint, and Ethical Dilemmas

The most controversial correctional psychiatry practices are the use of solitary confinement and physical restraint. Such measures commonly control violence, self–injury, or disruptive behavior, but they carry much risk to mental health and raise serious ethical questions (Haugom et al.,

2019). Correctional placement-based forensic psychiatrists must be highly cautious in their evaluation of the use of such interventions and lobby alternatives that will ensure safety and due consideration of human dignity.

Solitary confinement is a form of incarceration in which individuals are held in segregated housing units with minimal human contact and severe restrictions on movement, activities, and environmental stimulation. Such practices reduce threats, discipline, and protect those threatened(Haugom et al., 2019). However, long-term separation is likely to cause severe psychological upset. People exposed to long-term solitary confinement may suffer from psychiatric disorders. These effects are particularly harsh in people who have preexisting psychiatric conditions.

Psychiatrists often assess inmates in solitary confinement or advise on whether someone should be placed in or removed from isolation. Ethical responsibility requires the psychiatrist to balance institutional security with clinical well-being.

In many cases, solitary confinement acts as a substitute for mental health treatment. Facilities lacking psychiatric beds place suicidal or psychotic individuals in segregation under the label of "protective custody" or "administrative separation." While this prevents immediate harm, the lack of meaningful social contact and stimulation leads to rapid deterioration. Forensic psychiatrists should recognize these risks and demand alternative solutions such as therapeutic hosting, increased monitoring, or even hospitalization.

Physical restraint is used in prisons to control prisoners whose behavior is deemed risky or out of control. These include cuffs, shackles, restraint chairs, and four-point restraints. Although restraints apply as a defense against immediate danger or self-injury, they pose major medical and ethical dilemmas. Misuse of restraints is likely to cause physical injury, psychological trauma, or death(Haugom et al., 2019). The prolonged or repeated use of restraints may exacerbate psychiatric conditions, particularly in patients who have a history of trauma.

Psychiatrists decide, oversee, or evaluate the appropriateness of restraints in use. Restraints should be implemented only when necessary, for the quickest possible time, and under constant observation. Documentation shall provide details about when and how to restrain, the steps taken to achieve this, the total duration of the restraint, and the patient's experience. The American Psychiatric Association should administer restraints for disciplinary or administrative convenience. Restraints are only indicated for therapeutic purposes and not for discipline.

Ethical dilemmas are intrinsic to correctional psychiatry outside of solitary confinement and restraint. In most cases, forensic psychiatrists have to work within systems where the establishment's desires typically supersede patients' care needs. For instance, a psychiatrist might see a reason to transfer a patient to a psychiatric hospital, but containment procedures are crucial for the custody staff. Sometimes, custody staff may argue for placing a patient in a high-security unit, disregarding their mental susceptibilities(Haugom et al., 2019). The role of forensic psychiatrists is to make clinical judgments that are free of administrative pressures.

Correctional settings are a fundamental ethical dilemma due to double loyalty demands. Patients' welfare, as perceived by society, should match the requirement for order and control in correctional facilities, forming a task for psychiatrists. Patients must know that under administrative things, confidentiality may change, and authorities should tell them so.

Informed consent presents another dilemma. There are numerous occasions when authorities force prisoners to participate in a treatment or assessment. A psychiatrist has to make sure that patients make free and unintimidated treatment decisions. Respecting the autonomy of individual patients in treatment planning, unless in legally exceptional cases, is necessary. Making patients take their treatment into their own hands, as much as possible, given the limitations, is the main work of psychiatrists.

Several correctional centers have adopted alternative measures to enhance adequacy in solitary confinement and restraint procedures. Standing out are therapeutic housing units, mental health–specific pods, and plans for structured behavior support. Psychiatrists add value through clinical strategy design, staff competency improvement, and assessment of the effectiveness of these mechanisms. The efforts to reduce isolation and apply beneficial behavior support improve mental health outcomes and reduce the risk of harm.

Solitary confinement and physical restraint are dangerous matters and are riddled with serious ethical issues. Expert knowledge binds forensic psychiatrists to do their best to diminish harm, cultivate ethical care, and advocate for less harmful practices. Ethics and clinical judgment are pivotal elements that help the psychiatrist intelligently provide help to the correctional aspect. Psychiatrists attain this balance by matching risks to inform policy and provide compassionate care that respects patients' fundamental rights.

6.3 Medication Management and Treatment Resistance in Incarcerated Individuals

Psychiatric medication is one of the most frequently used tools for managing mental illness in correctional settings. In jails and prisons, where access to psychological therapy is limited, medications often form the foundation of mental health care. However, prescribing and managing these treatments in incarcerated populations presents unique clinical, legal, and ethical challenges(Howes et al., 2021). Forensic psychiatrists must navigate treatment resistance, non-adherence, misuse, side effects, and involuntary medication procedures, all while maintaining the trust and protecting patient rights.

Medication management begins with accurate diagnosis and appropriate selection of treatment. Incarcerated individuals may present with severe psychiatric conditions, including schizophrenia, bipolar disorder, and major depression. According to Baillargeon et al. (2009), approximately 14% of male and 31% of female inmates in U.S. state prisons have a diagnosed mental disorder, and most receive some form of psychotropic medication. These numbers are likely similar or higher in systems where community mental health care is inaccessible or overstretched.

Prescribing in correctional facilities is affected by various constraints. Limited formularies restrict access to the most effective or better-tolerated medications. Psychiatrists encounter pressure to choose cheaper options or avoid medications considered high risk for addiction, such as benzodiazepines or stimulants. Under-treatment and inconsistent access to drugs are common in correctional institutions, particularly those with overcrowding or limited psychiatric staff.

The aspect of resistance to therapy is also a significant concern. The refusal to take medication in incarcerated people may be due to such reasons as lack of insight, fear of side effects, firm religious beliefs, or distrust of staff at the clinic.

It is essential to understand what motivates non-adherence before experts in psychiatry try to eliminate resistance. According to Howes et al. (2021), a few patients forego medication because of fears that the drugs may cause weight gain, drowsiness, or sexual side effects. Some people have received coercive care in the past, and they use medication aversion as a defense. Communication, education, and involving patients in care decisions may help decrease non-adherence. Participatory decision-making promotes a more stable therapeutic alliance and increased compliance, even with those under forensic care.

In correctional facilities, employees may practice strict control of medication, crushing, or the physical state of drug modification. These tactics reduce the chances of diversion but could also occur by surprise and elevate mistrust while lessening treatment results. Achieving a balance in treatment goals between safety and autonomy is one of the significant tasks of forensic psychiatry, as it involves everyone's interest. Long-acting injectable (LAI) treatment represents an effective way to prevent misuse and ensure compliance in patients with reduced insight or erratic behavior.

The section on involuntary treatment requires specific challenges within the treatment. Sometimes, when patients refuse medication for their safety or others' grounds, psychiatrists have no option but to rely on legal protocols to force their treatment. Regulations differ across jurisdictions but require legal proceedings, psychiatric assessments, and short-term orders. Psychiatrists can offer medication against patients' unwillingness if they are not able to, but the decision pursues their best interests. However, some measures are essential for potential misuse prevention.

Capacity determination forms an integral part of such assessments. The psychiatrist should examine whether the person understands the condition, the reasons for suggested treatment, and the probable consequences of refusing medical care. Recording should include the patient's reasons for refusing treatment, pertinent clinical observation, and efforts to obtain voluntary agreement. Keeping the procedure open and equitable preserves the individual's dignity and reduces the suffering associated with compulsory treatment.

The correctional authorities must monitor the side effects of medications closely because many prisoners cannot afford regular medical checks or attention. Issues often include metabolic syndrome, extrapyramidal symptoms, and cardiac disorders. Howes et al. (2021) state that routine monitoring of weight, blood sugar, fat, cholesterol levels, and vital signs is required. Comprehensive care is sometimes difficult owing to overcrowded settings and unstable staffing. Forensic psychiatrists should advocate for implementing monitoring standards and work with medical teams to ensure patient safety.

So, clear communication between the psychiatrist, custody personnel, and patients about medications is paramount. Members of the custody team can deal with medication dispensation and determine how inmates behave. Providing them with those skills to identify psychiatric indicators, consider drug side effects, and understand drug functions can make a difference. So, the number of potential disputes is reduced, and patients obey their medication plans.

Care after their release needs to be seamless for patients. Many ex-inmates are discharged without medication or with coordination for future appointments. Lack of adequate support increases the chances of relapsing, becoming a homeless person, or committing new crimes when discharged. Forensic psychiatrists have the tasks of planning, drug provision, and networking with community care providers. Giving "warm" handovers to mental health services through linkage programs reduces recidivism and improves long-term outcomes.

Clinical expertise, ethical decision-making, and contribution to the system improvement allow forensic psychiatrists to provide empathetic and efficient care. In addition to writing medications, forensic psychiatrists must educate patients, monitor their progress, work with them, and supervise the general direction of care. Good medication management in corrections increases recovery and patient safety and improves rehabilitation outcomes.

6.4 Summary and Takeaways

Correctional psychiatry is one of the most challenging aspects of forensic mental health. Those in correctional environments tend to have mental illnesses, addiction, and trauma experiences, but their treatment occurs in environments that prioritize security over therapeutic intervention. Forensic psychiatrists provide competent services related to mental health in settings that pose safety challenges and lack available resources.

In the introductory part of the chapter, the emphasis was on mental health care delivery within jails and prisons. It highlighted the need for timely screening, adequate diagnosis, and consistent care. There are both medical needs of the patients and correctional system limitations involved in providing mental health services in prisons and jails. Psychiatrists are usually also limited by funding, staff shortages, and resistance from the inmates and the construction of the system.

Solitary confinement and physical restraints are serious ethical issues. These interventions exacerbate psychiatric symptoms and infringe patient's autonomy, particularly when applied to those with mental illness. Psychiatrists need to promote safer alternatives and make sure that any restrictive measures are medically justified, time-limited, and well-documented.

Medication management is central but complex. Treatment resistance, misuse of medication, and non-adherence form are common. Psychiatrists must evaluate capacity, control side effects, and cooperate with the custody people. Involuntary treatment must be conducted under legal cover, and discharge must be part of a plan to link the patient to community care. Forensic psychiatrists in corrections need clinical acumen, ethical clarity, and system-level leadership. Through adherence to patient rights, humanistic practices, and evidence-based care, they boost outcomes in a vulnerable, often ignored population.

Chapter 7: Child and Adolescent Forensic Psychiatry

Child and adolescent forensic psychiatry is concerned with the overlap between mental health and the legal aspects of the minor. This discipline requires a specific approach that entails a clinical understanding of childhood development, knowing the legal issues, the sensors of the family, and social dynamics. Boonmann et al. (2024) state that while society believes adults understand and maneuver legal regimes with rational thought, children and adolescents cannot be assumed to be the same. Young people's minds and emotions are still developing, which has a bearing on their understanding, responding, and getting involved in legal proceedings.

This chapter deliberates upon three main areas of child and adolescent forensic psychiatry. Juvenile fitness to stand trial and waiver to adult court, child custody evaluations, and trauma assessments involved in cases of abuse and neglect. These are the areas that demonstrate the central role that forensic psychiatrists play in ensuring children's voices, vulnerabilities, and mental health needs are correctly heard and represented in legal settings. Each part will detail essential considerations from a clinical and legal perspective, the evaluation matter, and ethical obligations that psychiatrists should follow.

7.1 Juvenile Fitness to Stand Trial and Waiver to Adult Court

Juvenile Fitness to Stand Trial (FST) evaluations represent one of the key roles of child and adolescent forensic psychiatry. According to Kruh et al. (2022), these evaluations help establish whether minors have the mental ability to appreciate court proceedings and contribute effectively to their defense. Although adults are supposed to have such abilities, children and adolescents should be given special consideration because of the continuous growth of their cognitive and emotional lives.

Age, maturity, and life experience are the factors that usually hinder a juvenile's understanding of the legal system. Many cannot define such legal roles as "prosecutor" or "defense attorney" or know their rights and the long-term consequences of the legal decisions. Children may learn they are in trouble without knowing what trial is about or how to work with their lawyer. Therefore, the evaluation of FST in young people cannot but include persons' developmental stages of life, their communication competencies, mental well-being, and suggestibility.

The initial step in the evaluation process is a comprehensive developmental and psychological assessment. According to Kruh et al. (2022), psychiatrists should assess intellectual functioning, attention span, memory, and reasoning. Symptoms of mental health, including psychosis, depression, or anxiety, could further hinder a child's ability to participate in the legal process. Clinicians often have to simplify questions and use images for younger children. The interview has to be supportive and noncomplaining, in which children are able to express themselves freely and without fear.

Apart from the assessment of FST, courts occasionally ask for evaluations so that a juvenile case can be sent to an adult criminal court. This legal action, commonly referred to as a waiver, applies to older adolescents who have committed serious or violent crimes. Individual decisions for waiver are based on the age of the minor, history of previous offenses, treatment history, and the nature of the alleged crime. While the juvenile court has a rehabilitation orientation, the adult court tends to be more punitive. Thus, the consequences are more severe for the youth involved.

When evaluating waivers, forensic psychiatrists do not judge the mental health of those tested but rather developmental maturity, rehabilitation, and tendencies toward future offending. According to Bullough et al. (2021), the emphasis is on the youth's ability to accrue something from treatment and positively change their behavior. Impulse control, problem-solving skills, empathy, and sensitivity to authority figures are the areas that evaluators elaborate upon. Risk factors such as peer influence, family dysfunction, and substance use need also to be taken into account.

Suggestions made in FST and waiver cases should be in a manner that is comprehensible to legal experts and the court in reports. The psychiatrist should be impartial, depend on facts, and avoid choosing emotions or speculating. Such reports are essential in courts and help to make sure the public is secure while giving young people the possibility to grow and change.

7.2 Child Custody Evaluations

Evaluations of child custody are essential in forensic psychiatry involving children and adolescents, and they are usually requested in the context of divorce, separation, or debates about guardianship. Chung et al. (2020) explain that these evaluations provide the court with unbiased, trained opinions about family, parenting, and the child's needs. The objective is not to decide who the best parent is but to choose a custody arrangement that supports the child's safety, security, and intense emotions.

Custody cases can bring about a lot of intense feelings. Any distress, anger, or grief expressed by parents can affect their behaviors and thoughts. On the other hand, children end up in the middle, fearful to express their wishes or be loyal to one parent more than to the other. Forensic psychiatrists should approach these evaluations with objectivity, strict clinical observations, and an awareness of each individual family's context.

The evaluation process normally involves one-on-one interviews with each parent and the child, observing their interactions, and gathering collateral information. Collateral sources are school records, health documents, previous psychological assessments, and information on pediatricians or childcare workers. Every piece of information helps to create a full image of the child's life and relationships.

Some of the important areas examined include the ability of each parent to provide emotional support, consistency, structure, discipline, and access to healthcare and education. Chung et al. (2020) state that the parent's mental health and history of substance use, ability to communicate and resolve conflicts, and willingness to support the child's connection with the other parent are all assessed by the psychiatrist. High conflict cases such as abuse allegations or alienation cases require special effort at assessment.

The evaluation highly emphasizes the child's perspective. Whether children are interviewed alone or with a parent depends on their age and level of development. The psychiatrist should establish trust and explain the process using age-appropriate language. No child should ever "choose" between parents, but he or she can state preferences or describe experiences. These views are vital but are never independent of developmental needs and family context.

It gives crucial insights into interactions. For instance, are the parents' responses sensitive to the cues made by the child? Is the child relaxed and secure, fearful and withdrawn? How does the parent discipline or change the behavior? These observations in real time may correspond to or be contrary to what parents mention when interviewed.

Cultural, religious, and socioeconomic factors affect parenting practices and must be considered carefully. Depending on the viewer, a form of discipline may appear harsh when it might be the norm and acceptable in other cultural contexts. Separating culturally-based practices and practices that present real dangers to the child's well-being are functions that the forensic psychiatrist has to perform.

The issue of special attention is in cases where parents are suffering from mental illnesses or personality disorders. According to Robb (2023), the fact that the parents have a diagnosis does not mean they are unfit. Instead, the evaluator assesses how symptoms impact parenting behavior, decision-making, and emotional availability. In the same way, an expert should also examine a history of substance abuse concerning current behaviors, engagement in treatment, and potential for relapse.

The final report should be well structured and to the point to answer the court's questions. It should summarize relevant findings; evaluate their impact on the child's development, and recommend custody and visitation issues. It has to use objective language free from inflammatory and judgmental expressions. All that should be considered in the best interest of the child.

In certain jurisdictions, psychiatrists testify to what they have come up with. In front of a judge, the experts need to account for why they arrived at their opinions, justify their methods, and answer the cross-examination. In such settings, one should be confident, clear, and honest. The psychiatrist should not speculate but stay within the collected data during the evaluation.

7.3 Trauma Assessments: Abuse and Neglect

Trauma assessments in abuse and neglect cases are one of the most delicate and critical aspects of child and adolescent forensic psychiatry.

According to Silva et al. (2024), the experts frequently request such assessments during Child Protection investigations, custody disputes, or when they bring criminal charges against somebody for causing harm. The psychiatrist's job is to evaluate the extent of mental damage due to abuse or neglect to the child, to assess current mental health needs, and to provide recommendations that help maintain their safety and recovery.

Abuse comes in different forms, physical, sexual, and emotional, and leaves its mark on psychological scars. Deprivation of food, access to medical amenities, education, or emotional nurturing by neglect can be no less harmful, particularly if sustained over time. According to Silva et al. (2024), trauma appears in obvious forms of fear, aggression, sadness, or in a subtler manner through withdrawal from activities, sleep disorders, academic failure, or regression in speech. Not all children will come out to express themselves directly, particularly when young or frightened and manipulated by caregivers.

When conducting trauma assessments, one starts with a clinical interview and observation. The psychiatrist must gain trust and ensure the children realize why they are evaluating them. The tone has to be supportive, non-threatening, and age-appropriate. Drawing, toys, or play-based interviews are good for young children to express themselves. Teenagers need confidentiality and safety before anyone can expect openness from them.

The primary ethical responsibility is not to use leading or suggestive questioning. Forensic trauma assessments are not therapy. They gather accurate information while not violating the child's rights, avoiding memory distortion, and encouraging confabulation. According toAlkema et al. (2024), the psychiatrist must be impartial and leave the child to narrate occurrences at his will and in his own words. Open-ended question prompts are better than direct or emotionally charged questions.

Besides the interview, an in-depth assessment involves perusing collateral information. It includes school performance reports, medical and psychological records, previous child protection reports, and the input of teachers, relatives, or pediatricians. Behavior patterns, past injuries, and history (related to the caregiver) come into play when constructing an elaborate portrait of the kid's experience.

The psychiatrist should be calm and document the disclosure properly when a child engages in abuse or neglect disclosure. Most mandatory reporting legislations require that any reasonable suspicion of abuse be reported to the relevant authorities immediately. Alkema et al. (2024) state that it is essential to explain to the children, in language appropriate to their age, that they must share some information with others to protect them. Honesty regarding this process creates trust, which prepares the child for what is to come next.

In most cases, evaluation also involves determining the caregiving environment. This entails interviewing parents/guardians to assess their mental state, parenting skills, insight into a child's needs, and motivation to perform protective action. For the caregiver accused of abuse or neglect, the psychiatrist needs to determine whether he/she can admit harm, take responsibility, and modify behavior. These insights enable the courts to decide whether reunification should be the option or they should seek other arrangements.

Evaluating the children's protective characteristics and resistive abilities is equally essential. No child will react to a trauma in the same manner. According to Silva et al. (2024), some children have good coping mechanisms, good relationships with non-abusive adults, and/or positive experiences at school, which help shield them from the adverse effects. The psychiatrist must discover, promote, and expand on these aspects in the recommendations.

The final report should effectively connect the child's symptoms, behavior, and history to the worries of the court or agency. It should detail the probable impact on the psychological aspect of the reported experiences, the mental state of the child, and the potential dangers of relocating back into the previous life environment. Some recommendations include therapy, parental support, medical assistance, educational intervention, or supervised visitation. Psychiatrists should not use speculative language but make assumptions based on observable evidence. Sometimes, the psychiatrists give evidence in court, or they have to compose follow-up reports as new details are uncovered. However, consistency, clarity, and compliance with ethical standards are forever crucial in any communication.

7.4 Ethical Practice and Communication with Minors

Child and adolescent forensic psychiatry consists of ethical practice and good communication. Minor evaluations are different from adult evaluations in crucial aspects. According to Disla de Jesus et al. (2022), children are more susceptible, have changing cognitive abilities, and are usually dependent on grown-ups, who can also be victims of inquiry. These complexities put forensic psychiatrists in a precarious situation of balancing legal responsibilities, clinical neutrality, and the growth needs of the child.

The first ethical requirement in any forensic assessment of minors is obtaining informed consent and assent. In almost all legal systems, there has to be a parent or legal guardian who consents to the evaluation. Nevertheless, involving the kids and asking for their assent is also crucial-an age-appropriate agreement to participate.Disla de Jesus et al. (2022) state that even young children of six and seven years of age may be capable of explaining why they are seeing a psychiatrist, what will occur at the meeting, and how their information will be used. Assent enhances transparency, honors the child's developing autonomy, and creates a basis of trust.

Confidentiality is another critical issue. Confidentiality promotes freedom in therapeutic settings. However, in forensic settings, the evaluation is not confidential in its usual form. Information kids give during the review will be passed to courts, lawyers, or child protection authorities. The psychiatrist should explain this blatantly at the beginning of the review (Disla de Jesus et al., 2022). Children should know that although the psychiatrists are on their side to hear and understand them, what they tell them will be used to help others decide on their care, safety, or legal position. This knowledge will help avoid expectations that might lead to perceptions of betrayal or confusion later on.

One of the foundations of ethical forensic activity is avoiding dual roles. A psychiatrist who examines children for legal reasons should not treat them. If, for instance, evaluators take on the role of being therapeutic by probing too practically, they may prompt a conflict of interest, confusion concerning confidentiality, and an impression of conflict of interest. In high-conflict custody cases, the psychiatrist needs to have firmly set boundaries. The evaluator has to be taken by all the parties and the court to be neutral and objective.

Communication must be modified to one consistent with the child's maturity. Complex legal language, abstract thinking, or feelings-charged questions can easily intimidate or baffle younger children, making it difficult for them to understand what is being asked. Where needed, the psychiatrist should speak simple language, use visual aids, or use play-based methods. For instance, through dolls, drawings, or picture stories, a child can express emotions or describe relationships without depending on verbal skills. On the other hand, teenagers tend to react well to respectful and direct communication that considers their developing sense of independent life.

Cultural and linguistic sensitivity is essential. Children differ in expressions and reflect their family norms, traditions, or language. Children may not make eye contact not because of shame or guilt but because it shows respect in their culture. According to Hiriscau et al. (2016), the psychiatrist should take time to learn about the child's background and not force assumptions. In case language is a barrier, a qualified interpreter should be employed, not a family member or an untrained staff member. Miscommunication alters the meaning, breaks rapport, and brings unsound conclusions.

In forensic environments, kids could be defensive, withdrawn, or suspicious. They can be instructed on what to say or warned, not to mention some information. Perhaps they had previous interviews and experienced that they were invasive or confusing. The psychiatrist has to be patient and non-judgmental (Hiriscau et al., 2016). Establishing a safe and calm environment makes the child feel heard without pressure or fear. Notice of such nonverbal clues as posture, eye contact, or tone may provide information about the children's emotional state or the degree of their comfort.

Fair reporting is a part of ethical evaluations. The observations made by psychiatrists need documentation as accurately as possible and should not include personal opinions or unfounded conclusions. Reports should address behaviors, statements, and psychological patterns pertinent to legal issues. They should not guess on matters that do not fall in the sphere of the work of a psychiatrist. In talking about sensitive topics like abuse, neglect, or parent conflict, the psychiatrist needs to be cautious about any language construction that might be accusatory or dismissive.

Psychiatrists have to be ready to lobby for the proper treatment if needed. Although the primary role assigned is evaluative, psychiatrists who discover urgent mental health requirements, that is, suicidality, untreated psychosis, or exposure to ongoing danger, are obliged to report the concern and facilitate the necessary action. The ethical regimen involves the balancing of the position of an individual as a neutral evaluator and the professional obligation to avoid harm.

7.5 Summary and Takeaways

Child and adolescent forensic psychiatry is essential in the legal systems in that it offers expert assessments that consider the developmental, psychological, and emotional needs of minors. Regardless of whether the issue at hand is determining fitness to stand trial, suggesting custody arrangements, or evaluating the impact of trauma, forensic psychiatrists offer dispassionate, clinically based information to guide courts toward the making of informed and child-oriented judgments.

This chapter has dealt with four major areas: assessments for fitness to stand trial, waiver to adult court, child custody examinations, and trauma assessments in cases of abuse and neglect. Each jurisdiction is a separate entity in which specific approaches to solving the task are required, harmoniously combining legal criteria with children's age, mental state, and environment. Ethical practices such as clear communication, informed assent, cultural competence, and professional neutrality should be essential at every step.

The forensic psychiatrist evaluates and also protects. Children involved in legal proceedings are some of the weakest members of society. With their thoughtful, respectful, and evidence-based assessments, the psychiatrists contribute to the moral making of these young people so they are seen, heard, and treated justly. Their activity encourages the legal system's fairness pursuit and the health and well-being of children and families.

Chapter Eight: Sex Offenders and Paraphilic Disorders

Forensic psychiatrists find sex offenders and those with paraphilic disorders sensitive because of the serious harm they cause and the attention their crimes attract. They tend to cause strong feelings, legal difficulties, and continued focus. Forensic psychiatrists are often asked to assess these individuals for risk, to give expert testimony in court, and to plan treatments to stop further harm. Unlike other areas of forensic work, these assessments must meet clinical, legal, and ethical standards. According to Kafka (2012), in paraphilic disorders, people have intense sexual desires or behaviors toward people who have not given their consent. Although not all people with paraphilias commit crimes, those who do usually require structured treatment and regular monitoring. Since repeat offenses are common, it is essential to use the proper methods to assess and manage them.

8.1 Sex Offenders' Risk Assessment

Forensic psychiatrists are often required to assess the risk that a person will commit another sexual offense. It is common for psychiatrists to assess people accused or convicted of sexual offenses to predict if they might commit another crime. The results of these assessments guide courts, parole boards, and treatment teams in choosing sentences, release conditions, supervision plans, and risk-reducing interventions. The results of risk assessments can be severe. Therefore, they should be done carefully, fairly, and using the best information available. It involves using both clinical knowledge and set tools to help make decisions that can be explained and supported.

There are many types of sexual offending. Some sexual offenses involve physical contact, such as rape or sexual assault, while others are non-contact offenses, such as exhibitionism, voyeurism, or possession of child sexual abuse material. Offenders may choose to target adults or children. According to Chen et al. (2014), offenders might be people the victim does not know or knows well, such as a family member. They can be different in age, gender, background, and past psychological experiences. It is obvious from these differences that sex offenders cannot be described by just one profile. As a result, risk assessment should be personalized for every person and not depend on general ideas or stereotypes.

Assessing risk should be done using a planned and evidence-based approach. When assessments are not based on structure or standards, they are biased, unreliable, and hard to explain in court. Psychiatrists often rely on actuarial and structured professional judgment tools to help them find known risk factors for sexual recidivism. These tools result from years of research and help psychiatrists always create the same and dependable evaluations.

The Static-99 is one of the most commonly used actuarial tools. This scale was created for adult males who have been convicted of at least one sexual offense. The Static-99 is based on factors that do not change, for example, age, a person's criminal background, the type of victim, and their relationships. Every item is given a score, and the sum of the scores is used to estimate the chance of recidivism. Those who score higher are more likely to commit another sexual offense. The Static-99 is valuable because it gives a transparent and objective measure of risk. Nevertheless, it does not consider how things change over time, the effects of treatment, or the help available in different situations.

Many experts also rely on tools that assess dynamic risk factors to overcome this issue. The Stable-2007 looks at factors that are generally stable but could change, such as impulsivity, sexual preoccupation, problems with intimacy, and attitudes that support sexual offending. However, the Acute-2007 looks at factors that can change quickly and may suggest risk is about to happen, such as emotional collapse, access to victims, or substance abuse. Using these three tools allows for a better understanding of the person's risks and chances of improvement.

A valid risk assessment depends on having accurate information. Forensic psychiatrists should collect information from various sources. Tully et al. (2013) state that the action means interviewing the offender, checking their criminal history, reading police reports, and looking at their treatment records. Information from family members, schools, or past therapists helps explain how a person's behavior has changed over the years. In prisons, how a person behaves, for example, breaking the rules, being aggressive, and interacting with others, can show how ready they are to rejoin society.

Juvenile sex offenders must be treated differently. Unlike adults, children and adolescents are still growing in their thinking, feelings, and social skills, and sometimes, their actions are shaped by the influence of others, their age, or something they have experienced. Risk tools for juveniles are not the same as those for adults and usually look at family life, school performance, past experiences as a victim, and how well a juvenile controls their emotions. It is necessary to avoid giving young offenders labels that could harm their future because their risk level can often decrease with proper help.

The assessment relies on the psychiatrists' judgment even when using standard tools. Risk scores are not the last word on the subject. Instead, they should help form an opinion considering a person's past experiences, behavior, and abilities. For instance, a person with a high Static-99 score could have received years of intensive therapy, apologized sincerely, and formed a good support network. In contrast, people with a low score might look cooperative but do not change their attitudes. Psychiatrists should look at the data within the context of the patient's situation and not rely too much on numbers.

Risk assessments should also outline practical strategies for dealing with risks. Among these are suggestions for supervised release, electronic monitoring, treatment programs, and avoiding unsupervised contact with at-risk people. The evaluator should describe how each strategy addresses the individual's risk factors. Just calling someone "high risk" is not sufficient (Tully et al., 2013). The report should explain what it means regarding actions, the chance of repeating the offense, and the period being considered. In this way, the risk of something happening right after release could be higher, but it tends to decrease with age and steady living.

It is also essential to communicate about risks. The report should be well-organized, simple to read, and without any emotional or critical language. Since courts, parole boards, and similar authorities are not trained in psychiatry, it is necessary to explain psychiatric findings in a way everyone can understand. People should be told in plain language what "moderate risk" or "above average risk" means for their care, such as the requirement for supervision, treatment, or regular monitoring.

Risk is something that can change over time. People can change a lot when they receive the right help and support. When sentenced, individuals seen as high risk may be much less likely to commit another crime after receiving therapy, getting involved with their families, and behaving well for years. For this reason, risk assessments should be checked and updated regularly, mainly at critical times such as parole hearings and when a person is released from treatment. As a result, the system can adjust to changes, help with rehabilitation, and still keep the public safe.

Phallometric testing is another critical way to assess sex offenders. The test is used to understand the sexual interests of people who have been accused or convicted of sexual crimes. According to Ciardha et al. (2017), in phallometric testing, the size of the penis is measured when the person is exposed to sexual content. They let practitioners spot sexual arousal patterns that might not be evident only by asking questions or by self-reports.

As Bickle et al. (2021) identified, many sex offenders distort or keep their offenses secret, which can render common assessment tools unreliable. If such cases occur, phallometric testing may reveal whether the person's statements are correct. If defendants say they have no sexual interest in kids, but the test demonstrates they get aroused by child-related pictures, the psychiatrist might suspect they are more likely to re-offend. Data analysis helps determine the best sentencing, treatment, and supervision approach.

Even so, there are ethical and practical problems with using phallometric testing. Certain critics are concerned that the test is too invasive and may not be accepted in conservative communities. The test should only be conducted by trained experts using established methods to prevent legal problems and maintain the subject's dignity. Still, phallometric testing is considered a reliable way to assess deviant sexual interests and helps understand the offender's risk and what treatment is needed.

In high-risk cases or when other assessment results are unclear, forensic psychiatrists should consider using phallometric testing. If used correctly, it helps ensure ethical and evidence-based management of sexual offenders.

8.2 Legal Frameworks for Managing Sex Offenders

Countries globally have established particular systems to handle offenders convicted of sex crimes. They try to stop future harm, ensure those found guilty are responsible for their actions, and occasionally encourage efforts to rehabilitate offenders. Sexual offenses tend to result in serious emotional and social problems for most victims, who are usually children, and they can leave long-lasting mental effects (Tully et al., 2013). As a result, government policies now provide for supervision and controls that last long after any sentences have been served.

These laws include listing specific individuals as sexually violent predators. They are intended for sex offenders whose risk of committing more sexual crimes is thought to be high because of some mental condition. Legal descriptions of sexually violent predators change from one jurisdiction to another. Still, the main point is that some people must keep receiving supervision when their sentences have been served(Russell &Darjee, 2013). Supervision is usually a civil commitment within a secure psychiatric place, lasting until the person is no longer considered a threat to society.

Typically, forensic psychiatrists advise whether a person should be labeled a sexually violent predator. Psychiatrists observe mental illnesses, check past situations, and predict the chance of another offense. Their evaluations include criminal and psychological record reviews, clinical interviews, and risk assessment tools(Russell &Darjee, 2013). The mental health expert is not there to determine guilt or innocence but to provide an objective opinion to help the court use the right laws and standards. They must ensure their findings are correct, fair, and ethical while evaluating.

Another common legal response is sex offender registration. Typically, offenders must register with law enforcement and provide information about where they live, work, and other personal details. Some parts of the registry are made public in some countries; in others, this information is confidential and only used by authorities. The registry helps law enforcement agencies track and monitor people who could be at risk. However, public notification laws have been controversial. Some say they improve community safety; others say they contribute to unnecessary social stigma, unemployment, and housing instability, which can increase the likelihood of reoffending. These concerns suggest that the community must be protected, but at the same time, the potential for successful reintegration must not be undermined.

The law can also manage the actions of sex offenders after prison by setting post-release restrictions. Sometimes, these conditions mean the individual is not allowed to attend school, visit parks, or use daycare centers. The court may decide on supervised visits with minors, limit their use of the Internet, or require them to be monitored electronically. Usually, these conditions are made based on the risk factors discovered during the individual's assessment(Russell &Darjee, 2013). The rules should be just, tailored to the person, and match the real danger, making it harder for offenders to find victims. If restrictions are not specific enough, they limit people's freedoms and are hard to apply.

In other countries, the law mandates that certain sexual offenses be punished with a minimum sentence. The same approach is taken for all, which shows society's disapproval of these actions. However, in other countries, low-risk people or those accused of minor offenses are offered diversion programs or deferred adjudication. These programs require offenders to attend therapy, be on probation, and be monitored by the law.

In addition, courts order the offender to participate in sex offender treatment programs, submit to regular psychological evaluations, and submit to polygraph testing. According to McCartan (2012), in more serious cases, the courts can order the person to take anti-libidinal medication or to be chemically castrated if the person's sexual urges do not change after treatment. Although doctors supervise these treatments and are usually court-ordered, they raise ethical questions about autonomy, consent, and human rights. Except where the law allows otherwise, such measures must always be guided by clinical necessity, legal authority, and informed consent.

Legal and ethical issues surround laws allowing civil commitment after someone is released from prison. Some argue that these laws punish people for their actions in the future, not for what they have done. Consequently, taking a preventive approach blurs the difference between justice and security. However, those who back these laws argue they are needed to safeguard the public, mainly when applied to individuals with a history of predatory actions or conditions that do not respond to treatment.

The way mental health professionals execute their work is affected by the rules and regulations of the law. Forensic psychiatrists must be familiar with the laws and rules for sentencing and their responsibilities in reporting in their region. According to McCartan (2012), the decision on whether people are released or sent to a facility and the type and level of supervision after release depends on their assessments. In some areas, mental health experts are required by law to warn those in danger or to inform the authorities if they believe someone is at serious risk. If these duties are not fulfilled, there may be legal consequences and penalties for the professional.

The rules here are not straightforward, so psychiatrists must be very careful, precise, and ethical. Their reviews should be just, address every area, and be based on the most recent best practices. They should be able to present their findings in a way that lawyers can understand and does not infringe on the individual's rights.

The rules for sex offenders vary from one country to another and are frequently updated and talked about. They are created to help maintain safety, fairness, justice, and respect for people's rights in the community. Forensic mental health professionals give the courts reliable and clinically accurate information to assist their decisions. Since public concern about sexual offenses is shaping laws, mental health professionals need to keep up, adapt, and remain committed to ethical behavior.

8.3 Treatment Challenges and Recidivism Prevention

Managing sex offenders is a challenging, sensitive, and demanding job in forensic psychiatry. It is difficult since it requires changing old behaviors, addressing significant psychological issues, and sometimes endangering the public. Schmucker and Lösel (2017) state that several offenders have unusual ideas about sex, intimacy, and relationships and do not always understand how their actions hurt others. Because society rejects them for their crimes, sex offenders often have a tough time getting treatment and rejoining society. Forensic psychiatrists and therapists are expected to address risks, protect the community, and support better behavior in these individuals.

A big problem in treating substance use disorders is when people deny or minimize their issues. Several sex offenders do not realize that what they have done is illegal. If the person is a teenager or has an intellectual disability, some believe the actions are consensual. According to Schmucker and Lösel (2017), the offenders think they were falsely accused or misinterpreted the situation. Many believe these things to avoid feeling guilty, ashamed, or getting into legal trouble. Not understanding the process is a significant barrier to improvement in therapy. Psychiatrists aim to help people recognize their behavior without making them feel threatened or uneasy. The purpose is not to embarrass the offender but to motivate them to start making changes.

Lack of motivation is another obstacle. A lot of sex offenders are required by law to attend treatment rather than choosing to do so by themselves. According to Barroso et al. (2019), the external pressure can cause superficial compliance, where the person attends sessions but does not engage with the material. In these cases, therapists have to use strategies that increase internal motivation. Motivational interviewing is one such technique that involves exploring the person's values, concerns, and goals in a supportive and non-confrontational way. This method promotes self-reflection and makes offenders think about the advantages of change. It is also essential to build a strong therapeutic relationship. When the therapist has a dual role of monitoring and reporting, they must still create a space where the person feels heard, respected, and supported.

Cognitive behavioral therapy (CBT) is the basis for most treatment programs for sex offenders. This method enables people to recognize distorted thinking patterns and high-risk situations and develop healthier coping strategies. Modules in CBT programs usually include managing impulses, building empathy, understanding victim impact, and developing prosocial attitudes. Therapy for individuals with paraphilic disorders (conditions characterized by intense and persistent sexual interests in objects, situations, or individuals that are inappropriate or harmful) must also include managing deviant fantasies and preventing acting out. Rather than suppressing thoughts and behaviors, these programs seek to help people take control of them.

Treatment is often in the format of group therapy. It enables people to help each other, share experiences, and practice new skills in a structured setting. Offenders can also be challenged to confront denial and accept responsibility in group settings. But group therapy is not for everyone. Those with high levels of shame, social anxiety, or psychopathic traits do not do well in group settings. Individual therapy is more appropriate for these individuals. Treatment should be individualized to meet the needs of each person, including age, intellectual ability, language, culture, and personal history.

Treatment is complicated by co-occurring mental health conditions. Many sex offenders also have mood disorders, anxiety, substance use problems, or personality disorders. If left unaddressed, these issues interfere with therapy and increase the risk of recidivism. For example, someone with untreated depression may become unmotivated and drop out of treatment. According to Grossi (2017), someone with substance dependence may be more likely to act impulsively or seek out high-risk situations. Treatment plans that cover the sexual behavior and the mental health of the patient work better than those that focus only on one concern.

In some cases, medication may be helpful. Hormonal agents and antidepressants can decrease sexual drive, fantasies, and arousal. Sometimes, these drugs are used with people who have uncontrollable urges or who are at high risk of reoffending. Medication can be a helpful tool, especially for those with paraphilic disorders, but it should never be used alone (Grossi, 2017). Psychological therapy, risk management, and ongoing support work best in combination with medication. Medical treatment must be closely monitored for side effects; compliance and informed consent are essential.

It is essential to consider the person's environment to help prevent them from reoffending. Support from others, a safe place to live and work, and the community's acceptance stop many from reoffending. Individuals who return to chaotic, rejected, or isolated places are more likely to commit another crime. Programs that assist with reentry can significantly improve the results for people trying to start over. Some reentry support includes learning life skills, using mental health services, finding jobs, and having mentors. Community supervision can help offenders remain on the right path and answer to their responsibilities.

Monitoring is necessary for preventing recidivism. Following up, assessing risks, and reviewing cases are used to detect any early problems. Sometimes, other programs depend on polygraphs, supervised internet use, or Global Positioning System (GPS) tracking to observe behavior. While these tools can be helpful, they should be used ethically and with appropriate safeguards. The individual's current behavior, support systems, and treatment progress should be reflected in risk assessments, which should be updated regularly (Grossi, 2017). There should be a clear relapse prevention plan before an individual is released from prison or treatment. This plan should include triggers, coping strategies, and the support network the individuals can turn to when they are stressed or tempted.

Sex offender treatment is never easy, and not everyone will respond to intervention. Despite many years of work, some are still considered high-risk. Even so, a lot of people can change. It has been found that treatment programs that use cognitive-behavioral methods and are well-supervised help reduce the number of repeat offenders. The best results are achieved when these programs offer therapy, accountability, and structure.

8.4 Summary and Takeaways

The most complex and sensitive challenges in forensic psychiatry are sex offenders and those with paraphilic disorders. The main goals in managing these individuals are to accurately assess risk, follow legal protections, and support treatment that will reduce the likelihood of reoffending. Working with sex offenders requires risk assessment. The Static-99 is one of several structured tools that provide consistent, evidence-based risk estimates. But these tools are not enough by themselves. In addition, psychiatrists must make professional judgments based on each person's history, behavior, and current environment. Findings must be communicated to legal authorities in a way they can understand and apply, and risk must be reassessed over time.

Regions have different legal frameworks, which often include registration laws, post-release restrictions, and civil commitment for sexually violent predators. The purpose of these legal tools is to protect the public, but they are ethically problematic because they lack fairness, privacy, and the potential for lifelong supervision. Forensic psychiatrists should be aware of the laws in their area and how to balance the interests of the public with those of the individual.

Treatment is not easy, but it is crucial. A lot of sex offenders claim they did nothing wrong or are not interested in changing. The best results are often achieved using cognitive behavioral methods and medication if necessary. Programs should also help people with co-occurring disorders and assist with their return to the community. A person's success depends on therapy, stable housing, supervision, and a supportive setting.

It is not only about avoiding urges to keep from repeating crimes. It should encourage people to live differently. Forensic psychiatrists participate in every part of the process, starting with assessment and diagnosis and ending with treatment and monitoring. They should ensure their work is fair and ethical and follows both science and the laws in their place of work.

Chapter Nine: Substance Use and Forensic Psychiatry

Using drugs or alcohol can change a person's thoughts, feelings, and actions, and if it results in legal issues, the outcomes can be severe and lasting. Many cases in forensic psychiatry involve people whose drug or alcohol use has affected their behavior or decision-making. Green et al. (2023) state that people may behave strangely when drunk or feel confused and upset when they are going through withdrawal. Some people have ongoing problems that make handling daily tasks and legal duties tough. Forensic psychiatrists are regularly asked to explain how substance use can change a person's actions, decisions, and mental health. It is not limited to identifying the problem; it also requires seeing the whole situation. It requires paying attention, being fair, and explaining how substance use relates to the discussed legal issues. The chapter discusses the importance of clinical, legal, and ethical knowledge in substance-related cases in forensic settings.

9.1 Intoxication, Withdrawal, and Criminal Behavior

Substance use can quickly change people's behavior, judgment, and ability to control their impulses. These acute states are often involved in criminal behavior, from property crimes and assaults to impaired driving, domestic violence, and homicide (Achilli et al., 2024). Forensic psychiatrists are commonly asked to determine if individuals' mental state, caused by substance use, played a role in their actions during the crime.

Intoxication means that a person has become temporarily impaired by the ingestion of alcohol or drugs. Intoxication with a substance and dose can produce euphoria, disinhibition, aggression, paranoia, hallucinations, or sedation. Intoxication can impair a person's ability to think clearly and make sound decisions; however, most legal systems distinguish between voluntary and involuntary intoxication. Most of the time, a person who willingly takes drugs or alcohol is not allowed to use this as a defense for their actions. It is believed that people should be held responsible for the results of their actions, including getting drunk and then committing a crime.

Forensic psychiatrists should assess how much the impairment affects the person and if it is related to the alleged crime. Sometimes, intoxication can lead to a reduced ability to understand, which may be taken into account during sentencing or mitigation. For example, a person who is severely intoxicated may be unable to form the specific intent required to commit certain crimes. In other cases, especially with chronic substance use, the psychiatric focus is on underlying conditions such as substance-induced mood disorders, personality changes, or cognitive decline.

When someone stops or reduces their substance use, they may experience severe psychological and physical symptoms during withdrawal. According to McFadden et al. (2021), agitation, tremors, hallucinations, irritability, or confusion can occur when withdrawing from substances such as alcohol, opioids, or benzodiazepines. In addition, severe withdrawal may result in seizures or delirium, which impairs reality testing and functional capacity. If a crime is committed by a person who is withdrawing from drugs, the forensic psychiatrist must assess if the symptoms played a role in the person's mental state.

In some cases, a person may use involuntary intoxication or intoxication caused by a medical condition as a legal defense. An unexpected drug reaction or accidental use often prevents someone from recognizing what happened. Since these situations are unusual, examples like these prove why ensuring both a medical and psychiatric review is necessary for forensic assessments.

If patients have paranoia, hallucinations, or mania due to substance use, it can be difficult to assess them. Symptoms can be seen during intoxication or withdrawal and can resemble main psychiatric disorders. To find out if the mental illness is substance-induced or primary, the forensic psychiatrist looks at the timing of the symptoms, how long they have lasted, the pattern of substance use, and how the person responds to stopping the substance (McFadden et al., 2021). An accurate diagnosis is essential for legal opinions regarding criminal responsibility, fitness to stand trial and future risk.

A forensic psychiatrist, in practice, will look at arrest records, listen to witness statements, read toxicology tests, review prior assessments by psychiatrists, and gather information through interviews with other relevant people. According to Achilli et al. (2024), it is necessary to learn about the person's usual state, their drug use, and if there are any other mental disorders involved. The psychiatrist must consider the cultural, legal, and systemic factors that influence how substance-related behavior is interpreted and addressed within the legal system.

In correctional programs, people battling substance use are usually given little treatment, and they may still deal with craving, withdrawal, or a desire for drugs. Displaying these symptoms can affect plea bargains, sentencing court orders, and observing probation. Forensic psychiatrists should support plans that focus on the medical and legal needs of those who commit crimes involving substances.

9.2 Drug Courts and Diversion Programs

The legal system uses drug courts and diversion programs to handle cases involving people charged with substance-related offenses. Rather than only using prison sentences, these programs try to keep people from reoffending by providing treatment and close monitoring. Forensic psychiatrists are essential in determining eligibility, checking how the program works, and advising on treatment and risk management.

Drug courts were created because it was recognized that many offenders have substance use problems that lead to their crimes. Brady et al. (2022) state that traditional methods in criminal justice do not usually deal with the main reasons behind crime, which leads to people being arrested, imprisoned, released, and committing crimes again. Drug courts aim to help find offenders who can benefit from treatment and direct them away from the usual court process. Most of the time, participation is optional and depends on meeting specific program requirements.

Different countries have their own rules, but usually, a person must have a history of substance use, not be violent, and agree to treatment. Many people charged with possession, theft, or impaired driving are often considered for bail. Individuals with serious mental illness, a history of violence, or who usually do not follow treatment may not be included. The forensic psychiatrist's assessment shows if the individual is able, willing, and stable enough to participate in the program (Brady et al., 2022). It means evaluating a people's thinking skills, mental health, risk of violence, and understanding of their substance use.

Participants in a drug court program are admitted and then follow a highly structured regimen of intensive supervision and clinical treatment. It usually involves regular court appearances, frequent drug testing, individual and group therapy, case management, and compliance monitoring. A judge, prosecutor, defense attorney, probation officer, case coordinator, and treatment providers are often part of the court team. The model used in the jurisdiction will determine whether forensic psychiatrists are consultants or direct service providers.

Treatment components are individualized to meet the needs of each person and may include cognitive behavioral therapy, motivational enhancement, relapse prevention, trauma-informed care, and medication-assisted treatment. According to Dickson-Gomez et al. (2022), integrated treatment or referral to specialist services is also provided for co-occurring mental disorders. Continuity of care and coordinated service delivery is a key strength of drug court programs, which improve engagement and outcomes.

It is closely monitored. Participants must attend treatment sessions, submit to drug screens, maintain housing or employment, and avoid new criminal charges. Reinforcement may be through praise, reduced supervision, or rewards. Conversely, if the offender does not comply, sanctions such as increased drug testing, brief incarceration, or program warnings may be imposed. It is not about punishment but accountability and behavioral change.

To graduate from drug court, a person must remain abstinent, complete treatment goals, and show stability. The legal agreement may result in successful participants' charges being reduced or dismissed. Forensic psychiatrists are often called upon to complete progress evaluations and outcome reports to assist the court in understanding each participant's treatment response, ongoing risk, and readiness for reintegration. Sometimes, if an individual does not meet program expectations with reasonable support, they may be referred for extended treatment or other services.

Similar principles apply to diversion programs that may happen at earlier stages in the legal process, such as pre-charge or pre-trial. These programs permit eligible individuals to avoid formal prosecution if they agree to treatment and supervision. Diversion may also be used in post-sentencing contexts, such as probation or parole planning (Dickson-Gomez et al., 2022). The forensic psychiatrist's role is to assess suitability, define treatment goals, and monitor progress. Although diversion models can differ widely, they all seek to decrease reliance on incarceration and increase recovery and public safety.

Public health experts believe that drug courts and diversion programs help reduce the number of people in prisons and give more people access to addiction treatment. People who go through drug courts are less likely to commit new crimes, spend less time in hospitals, and enjoy better health over the long run than those who go through regular criminal justice. The most effective results come from well-funded, culturally aware, and community-connected programs.

Ethics should not be ignored. The programs should be explained and chosen freely, with everyone knowing what is expected and what will happen if rules are broken. Forensic psychiatrists should ensure that people are not forced to agree because of the risk of going to prison (Dickson-Gomez et al., 2022). The rules of confidentiality within the law should be respected. The court must know about the patients' treatment and safety, not their personal life.

Cultural and systemic barriers can influence how much people participate and their success. Individuals from marginalized groups may struggle with poor medical care, unstable housing, or dealing with immigration issues. Forensic psychiatrists should pay attention to these factors and assist in fair planning for treatment. Addressing structural inequalities and ensuring all eligible people can participate in program design is necessary.

Forensic psychiatrists are also expected to design training and policy programs. Their understanding can influence the creation of program rules, how assessments are carried out, and the development of ethical standards. Being involved in case reviews, advisory groups, or quality improvement efforts allows psychiatrists to improve care for many patients and the system.

9.3 Capacity Issues in Substance-Induced Psychosis

Substance-induced psychosis is a challenging area where psychiatry and the law meet. According to Ricci et al. (2024), forensic situations lead to essential questions about a person's ability to decide, participate in court cases, or be held accountable for their actions. Forensic psychiatrists are regularly asked to determine if someone with psychosis caused by substance use can make decisions for themselves or others. It is crucial to tell symptoms that come from drugs or alcohol from those that are long-lasting mental health problems.

When someone uses substances, psychotic symptoms such as hallucinations, delusions, and disorganized thinking may appear during or shortly after use or withdrawal. According to Ricci et al. (2024), psychosis is often linked to using cannabis, amphetamines, cocaine, hallucinogens, alcohol (during withdrawal), and synthetic drugs such as phenylcyclohexylpiperidine (PCP) or Synthetic Marijuana (spice). The symptoms can be similar to those of schizophrenia or bipolar disorder, so it is hard to know if drugs or a primary psychiatric disorder causes the problem.

The timing of using substances marks substance-induced psychosis. The symptoms are often noticed soon after use and may disappear when the person stops. In some cases, people may still have symptoms for weeks, mainly if they use strong substances a lot. Tomašić et al. (2023) state that some drugs can cause psychotic symptoms to last in those using them regularly, even after they stop. Forensic psychiatrists review toxicology reports, listen to witness statements, and conduct collateral interviews to understand the timeline of the patient's symptoms.

Substance-induced psychosis can be evaluated for capacity in several legal situations. A common question is whether the person had the mental state needed to commit a crime at the time. If the offense took place while the persons were psychotic because of substance use, the forensic psychiatrist should determine if the individuals knew what they were doing was wrong (Tomašić et al., 2023). Most countries do not allow people to use intoxication as a reason for their actions. If psychosis lasts after the intoxication and looks like a primary mental disorder, it may help defendants claim insanity or diminished responsibility.

Another frequent situation is when the court assesses whether defendants can understand the charges, talk to their lawyer, and follow the court proceedings. Due to substance-induced psychosis, a person may have trouble concentrating, remembering things, judging reality, and communicating, making them unfit for a time. When this happens, forensic psychiatrists decide if the impairment will improve with abstinence or if it needs further treatment. Restoring fitness may require a short hospital stay, detoxification, and psychiatric care.

Many times, patients are unable to give their consent to treatment. If a person is having substance-induced psychosis, they may be taken to a hospital for urgent psychiatric or medical assistance. The forensic psychiatrist should determine if the person can understand the treatment, consider its results, and make a sensible decision. Acute psychosis can disrupt the process, mainly when the person does not understand their condition or is paranoid. If someone's capacity is reduced, care may have to be provided under mental health laws or emergency medical rules.

If psychosis is caused by substance use, it may result in assessments of guardianship, financial abilities, or the need for involuntary care. If someone has spent a lot of money because of paranoid thoughts or hallucinations, he/ she may be sent for an assessment of his/ her financial abilities (Tomašić et al., 2023). A person who has substance-induced delusions and refuses treatment that could save their life may need a court to decide on their care. When doing these evaluations, the forensic psychiatrist must look at a person's thinking skills, ability to tell what is real, judgment, and any ongoing risks.

It is important to differentiate primary psychotic disorders from those caused by substance use in every capacity assessment. When assessing a patient, forensic psychiatrists should look at the person's psychiatric history, when symptoms started, how they have progressed, and how substances have been used. When psychosis is linked to substance use and disappears after abstinence, it is more likely to be diagnosed as substance-induced. However, if the symptoms do not improve when sober or there is a consistent pattern of worsening function, it may be due to a primary disorder. It influences how conditions are diagnosed and the results of legal and treatment decisions.

Long-term management is another consideration. People who have psychosis while using drugs or alcohol are more likely to develop lasting psychiatric illnesses. Frequent episodes can lead to declining thinking skills, a drop in social life, and more legal issues. When making recommendations, forensic psychiatrists should look at the person's outlook, support network, and how well they follow treatment. Early action, informing patients, and treating both disorders are essential to prevent relapse and improve patient function.

It is necessary to describe the findings understandably. The report should state the capacity and relate the clinical findings to legal issues. The conclusions should be presented in a way that is relevant to the law and should recommend what steps are needed, such as treatment, supervision, or more evaluation.

9.4 Forensic Management of Dual Diagnosis: Substance Use and Co-occurring Mental Illness

Dual diagnosis occurs when someone has a substance use disorder and also suffers from mental illness,for example,schizophrenia, bipolar disorder, major depressive disorder, or a personality disorder. According to Krishnan and Ireland (2023), in many cases, forensic psychiatrists deal with comorbidity, which complicates both criminal and civil evaluations. People with dual diagnosis might act in unexpected ways, make unwise choices, not understand things well, and not stick to treatment or legal rules. As a result, people may commit crimes, face daily challenges, and be more likely to end up in the justice system. Forensic psychiatrists are expected to examine the situation, provide accurate diagnoses, and suggest helpful recommendations for decisions in both court and healthcare.

Substance use and mental illness tend to affect each other in both directions. Some individuals with mental illness use drugs or alcohol to help deal with their symptoms, which is known as "self-medication." Someone struggling with depression might use alcohol to feel better for a short time, and someone with schizophrenia might smoke cannabis to reduce their hallucinations. On the other hand, using substances for a long time can lead to or worsen psychiatric symptoms (Krishnan and Ireland, 2023). The prolonged use of certain substances or alcohol can lead to memory loss, mood changes, or psychosis. Because of these effects, it is often hard to know if the substance, the disorder, or both cause the symptoms.

Forensic psychiatrists determine how each disorder affects the behavior or ability. To do this, a psychiatrist must review the patient's medical and psychiatric history, talk to family or caregivers, and sometimes check toxicology results. It is crucial to consider the timeframes involved. If individuals still have psychiatric symptoms after stopping substance use, it is more likely that they have a mental illness (Green et al., 2023). If the symptoms appear only when the person is intoxicated or withdrawing and disappear when they stop using, they are most likely substance-induced. The evaluator needs to examine how long the problem has lasted, its pattern, and the person's usual functioning.

Those with dual diagnosis in the criminal justice system may be charged with violence, property crime, disturbing the public, or breaking probation rules. The way they act is often sudden, not well thought out, and influenced by psychosis or mood swings, which can be made worse by being intoxicated or withdrawing from drugs. Forensic psychiatrists are commonly asked to determine if someone is responsible for a crime, if he/ she can participate in a trial, and if he/ she is likely to commit another crime (Green et al., 2023). It becomes even harder to answer these questions when two conditions affect cognition, emotion, and behavior at the same time.

When assessing someone with a dual diagnosis for fitness to stand trial, it is essential to consider how each condition affects their understanding of the law and their ability to talk with their lawyer. Psychosis can lead to false beliefs about the law, and intoxication or withdrawal can make it hard for a person to remember, pay attention, or judge reality (Hancq et al., 2021). If depression is not treated, it can lead to hopelessness or passivity, which makes it hard for someone to participate. If the person is very sick, they may need to be stabilized in a forensic hospital or treatment center before being reevaluated. Often, both the mental illness and the substance use disorder must be treated together to restore fitness.

In criminal responsibility cases, it is essential to assess whether the dual diagnosis made it impossible for the persons to know what they did was wrong. In some cases, the insanity defense is not allowed if the mental issue was brought on by someone's own choice to drink or take drugs. Yet, if a major psychiatric illness was involved, especially in cases that were difficult to treat, legal protections could still be used. The forensic psychiatrist needs to tell the court how intoxication and psychopathology each played a role in the offense.

Dual diagnosis is frequently crucial in civil forensic cases when deciding on guardianship, consent to treatment, financial matters, and the need for involuntary psychiatric care. Those with dual diagnosis tend to lack insight and make poor decisions, mainly when their mental illness is not treated, or their substance use continues. Forensic psychiatrists may be required to assess if the person can look after themselves, understand the pros and cons of treatment, or handle money (Hancq et al., 2021). The evaluation should concentrate on what the persons can do on their diagnoses. While some people with dual diagnosis can function well with help, others may need to be supervised, cared for, or have a legal guardian.

Fitness for duty evaluations in workplaces may also include people with dual diagnosis. Healthcare, aviation, or law enforcement workers must be mentally stable and sober because their jobs are critical and require safety and sobriety. Suppose a person with a dual diagnosis is sent for evaluation because of unusual behavior, not showing up for work or poor performance. In that case, the forensic psychiatrist should check how both disorders affect their job. It means looking at the chance of relapse, how well the patient follows treatment, and whether they can return to work or need any accommodations.

Planning for treating people with dual diagnosis should be thorough and involve all relevant services. When care is divided between addiction services and mental health services, the treatment is often not well coordinated, and the results are poor. It is best to manage both conditions simultaneously, using a team of different experts (Hancq et al., 2021). Someone with a dual diagnosis may be treated with psychiatric drugs, medication-assisted therapy for substance use, cognitive-behavioral therapy, strategies to prevent relapse, and social support. Having a home, a job, and friends is essential for a lasting recovery.

Forensic psychiatrists participating in court-ordered treatment planning should support goals that can be accomplished. It means suggesting programs that can handle dual-diagnosis cases, address emergencies, track progress, and communicate with the legal system. Sometimes, a secure treatment setting or a conditional release plan is the best option. It is crucial to keep assessing risks regularly. People with dual diagnosis are more likely to engage in violence, self-harm, and suicide than those with only one diagnosis. It is essential to manage both the psychiatric causes and the substance-related actions in risk management.

9.5 Summary and Takeaways

Forensic psychiatry is greatly concerned with substance use disorders because they can influence criminal activity, legal choices, and mental health. Intoxication and withdrawal can make it difficult for people to think clearly and control their actions, which may result in offenses from stealing to violent crimes. Forensic psychiatrists assess if these states changed a person's ability to decide, control their behavior, or realize the outcomes of their actions. Even though voluntary intoxication is not usually an excuse for crime, it can be considered when deciding on risks and sentencing. Drug courts and diversion programs provide an alternative to jail, helping people recover, stick to their treatment, and be responsible. Forensic psychiatrists are essential in deciding if a person is eligible for the program, following their progress, and advising the court about clinical and risk issues.

A person with substance-induced psychosis may not be able to take part in a trial, agree to treatment, or handle everyday activities. Forensic psychiatrists are expected to tell apart symptoms caused by drugs from those due to mental illnesses, and their assessments should help with legal and medical decisions. In all these situations, the forensic psychiatrist acts without bias, ensuring that any substance-related problems are evaluated and handled appropriately. Their efforts encourage ethical choices, safeguard the public, and help people with addiction and mental health issues.

When a person has substance use and another mental illness at the same time, forensic assessments become more challenging. Many times, these individuals are more likely to have risks, face more legal issues, and have poorer results if they do not get integrated care. Forensic psychiatrists must explore the relationship between the disorders, verify the diagnoses, and advocate a treatment plan that addresses both mental and substance-related problems. Their skills allow them to make ethical and effective decisions in the most challenging cases in forensic work.

Chapter 10: Malingering and Deception

Malingering happens when a person pretends to have psychological or physical symptoms to gain something. Bellman et al. (2022) point out that it is essential but sometimes challenging to detect malingering in forensic psychiatry since some individuals may pretend to be ill to avoid facing criminal charges, getting disability benefits, affecting custody decisions, or avoiding workplace consequences. Malingering is not caused by any mental illness, unlike genuine mental illness, but is done to trick an evaluator or the legal system. Forensic psychiatrists are sometimes asked to assess if a person's symptoms are real or not. They require careful monitoring, the use of proper assessment tools, knowledge of how people typically lie, and the judgment of a professional. Naturally, misjudging someone as malingering or failing to notice deception can have significant consequences. This chapter focuses on how forensic psychiatrists identify malingering, spot common fake disorders, and follow ethical rules in reporting their findings to the law.

10.1 Detection Strategies

Malingering refers to deliberately producing fake or greatly exaggerated symptoms to gain something from the outside world (such as money, avoiding work or military service, avoiding legal responsibility, or getting access to drugs). Jayadi et al. (2024) point out that malingering is a unique issue in forensic psychiatry since it requires differentiating real mental illness from deliberate deception. Forensic evaluations differ from most clinical settings, where the primary goal is to help patients feel better; the primary goal of forensic assessment is to assess the truth, function, and responsibility. Suppose there is reason to suspect that someone is pretending to be ill for financial gain. In such cases, the forensic psychiatrist must approach them systematically, utilizing a range of tools and strategies to assess credibility and effort.

The first step in detecting malingering is to realize when the possibility should be considered. Malingering is not rare, but it is not universal. Deception can only be suspected if there is a solid reason supported by what is seen and heard during a session. Inconsistency between reported symptoms and observed behavior, a conflicting story from the individual, lack of cooperation during evaluation, or exaggerated or unusual symptom presentation are all suspicious indications of malingering (Jayadi et al., 2024). However, if individuals say that they are very psychotic, but the speech about the symptoms sounds too carefully rehearsed, then additional investigation may be necessary.

The context is also important. The chances of malingering increase in situations that benefit the person in some way or have a legal impact. People dealing with criminal hearings, applying for disability benefits, attending workers' compensation reviews, or taking part in custody cases might purposefully make their symptoms appear worse or lie about them. Conversely, malingering is less likely to occur in emergency or acute inpatient settings where hospitalization may lead to unwanted restrictions.

The forensic psychiatrist should always keep in mind the context of the evaluation and be alert to the possibility of motives for deception.

The detection of malingering remains a clinical observation. The psychiatrist can then assess the consistency, plausibility, and internal logic of the reported symptoms through a careful interview. According to Jayadi et al. (2024), malingerers may not know much about psychiatric disorders and may use stereotypes or what they have seen in the media. Consequently, their symptom descriptions may be overblown, vague, or inconsistent with known clinical patterns. For example, a person faking schizophrenia may report hearing voices all day long, without any fluctuation, or describe visual hallucinations that are more common in organic conditions than in psychotic disorders. Individuals pretending to be amnesic may also report forgetting basic facts inconsistently or unrealistically, but their general behavior is inconsistent with this.

The collateral information is also essential. The objective data against which reported symptoms can be compared includes medical records, school records, employment histories, and witness statements. Monaro et al. (2021) state that forensic psychiatrists should always review past evaluations, hospitalizations, or legal documents for discrepancies. When some people say they were psychiatrically hospitalized for months because of severe depression, but there are no records, it raises questions about the truth of their account. Likewise, if people say they cannot work because of panic attacks but they have been working without support, which is inconsistent.

Psychological testing plays a crucial role in detecting malingering. With validated tools, it is possible to see if someone is making an effort or if the symptoms are in line with real mental illness. According to Monaro et al. (2021), the Structured Interview of Reported Symptoms (SIRS) is a tool used to detect individuals who may be feigning mental health problems. The SIRS examines rare symptoms, unusual combinations of symptoms, and overuse of common symptoms to determine how strategies present symptoms. The SIRS scoring patterns can be used to identify individuals who may be exaggerating or fabricating their symptoms.

Another tool commonly used is the Minnesota Multiphasic Personality Inventory–3 (MMPI-3). The assessments include validity scales designed to detect unusual or exaggerated symptom reporting. The F-scale (Infrequency) measures responses infrequently endorsed by clinical populations, while the Fp-scale (Infrequency-Psychopathology) is more specific to exaggeration in psychiatric samples. Barbosa-Torres et al. (2023) posit that very high scores on these scales indicate that individuals are attempting to appear more disturbed than they are. However, high scores have to be taken with a lot of caution because people with real disorders will also score high because they are distressed or disorganized in their thinking.

Effort testing is critical in cases where cognitive impairment or memory loss is claimed. Performance Validity Tests (PVTs) are used to determine whether a person is exerting effort during neuropsychological testing. For example, the Test of Memory Malingering (TOMM) and the

Word Memory Test (WMT). These tests are easy enough that even individuals with cognitive impairments can perform above chance level. Intentional failure scores well below chance, which strongly supports a diagnosis of malingering. These tools are essential in forensic settings where claims of traumatic brain injury or dementia are common.

Another powerful indicator of malingering is behavioral inconsistency. Suppose people claim they cannot remember recent events but are observed moving around in their environment without difficulty, remembering appointments, or performing complex activities. In that case, their behavior does not match their words. Similarly, if someone claims to be too paranoid to be around others but is observed socializing in groups or interacting normally with staff, this discrepancy should be documented. These observations should be carefully noted by forensic psychiatrists and taken into account when they form their opinions.

In addition to formal tools and clinical observation, the forensic psychiatrist must also consider base rates and probabilities. According to Barbosa-Torres et al. (2023), the endorsement of certain symptom combinations is so rare in clinical populations that it strongly suggests fabrication. For example, individuals who endorse every possible symptom on a checklist or report nearly all symptoms as severe and unrelenting may not be presenting their condition realistically. The problem is that over-reporting can backfire, particularly when the symptoms described do not fit into any known diagnostic category or when they seem too numerous and intense.

However, it is essential to recognize that not all inconsistencies or unusual presentations are indicative of malingering. Some people may struggle to understand questions, have cultural or linguistic differences that affect communication, or may be disorganized in their thinking due to a real illness. As a result, malingering should never be diagnosed lightly. It must be based on a convergence of evidence, including behavioral observation, psychological testing, collateral data, and clinical judgment. It takes more than a single test result or inconsistency.

The forensic psychiatrist should also be careful to distinguish malingering from factitious disorder, in which symptoms are intentionally produced but without apparent external gain. In factitious disorder, the motivation is a psychological need to be sick, whereas in malingering, the motivation is for tangible rewards. It is essential for legal and ethical reasons. Malingering may be better addressed in legal proceedings, whereas factitious presentations may be better addressed in mental health treatment.

Malingering must be approached with even greater care when evaluating children or adolescents. Young people may exaggerate or fabricate symptoms to seek attention, escape, or protection, but they may also be developmentally unable to appreciate the consequences of their behavior fully (Barbosa-Torres et al., 2023). In these cases, the forensic psychiatrist should consider developmental level, history of trauma, and environmental influences before concluding intentional deception.

Finally, the forensic psychiatrist must clearly and objectively document all findings. If malingering is suspected, the reasons for this conclusion must be explained in detail, including specific behaviors, test results, and inconsistencies. Accusatory language should be avoided in reports, and only facts should be reported. Instead of calling someone a malingerer, phrases like "there is evidence suggestive of exaggeration" or "test results are not consistent with genuine cognitive impairment" are more appropriate. The findings are both defensible and ethically sound because of precise, measured language.

10.2 Common Feigned Disorders

Forensic psychiatrists need to know what types of disorders people often try to fake, the usual patterns and inconsistencies that suggest deception, and the clinical methods for detecting false or inflated presentations. Almost any disorder can be malingered, but some diagnoses are more commonly malingered because of their legal relevance or social recognition. Post-traumatic stress disorder (PTSD), cognitive deficits (especially memory impairment), psychotic disorders, and mood disorders are among the most commonly feigned.

Post-Traumatic Stress Disorder (PTSD)

In forensic cases, PTSD is a popular diagnosis for malingering since it is well-known, connected to severe distress, and may lead to receiving compensation or leniency in court. PTSD can be claimed by individuals in personal injury cases, when applying for asylum, in claims by veterans, or during evaluations for criminal responsibility (Al Jowf et al., 2023). Although PTSD is a severe and disabling illness for many, it is also easy to fake because symptoms are based on personal reports, and it is hard to prove the actual trauma.

In many cases, people pretend to have PTSD by experiencing intrusive memories, nightmares, and flashbacks, being overly alert, and avoiding certain situations. Malingerers might use exaggerated or stereotypical terms to describe their symptoms, often repeating things they have seen or heard on the internet or in the media. For example, they might say they have constant flashbacks that are always the same, or they might report having nightmares every night in the same way, which is not typical in real cases (Al Jowf et al., 2023). In addition, malingered PTSD usually does not include the usual functional problems or other symptoms that are common in true PTSD, such as emotional numbing, dissociation, and changes in how someone relates to others.

If the description of trauma is not clear, keeps changing or cannot be confirmed, it is another warning sign. When individuals' stories change frequently, their timelines are exaggerated, or their facts do not align with established knowledge, it may indicate that the trauma was fabricated (Kranenburg et al., 2023). Forensic psychiatrists ought to check the truth of the reported trauma, confirm details when they can, and investigate if the symptoms are the same in different interviews and from other sources.

Assessment tools such as the Clinician-Administered PTSD Scale (CAPS) or the M-FAST (Miller Forensic Assessment of Symptoms Test) are assessment tools that can help determine if a person's symptoms are genuine. If individuals score high on some validity scales, report unusual symptoms more frequently than others, and give inconsistent answers, it may suggest that they are exaggerating (Kranenburg et al., 2023). If a person shows little emotion when discussing upsetting matters or suddenly changes their mood, it can help the clinician make a more accurate diagnosis.

Cognitive Deficits and Memory Loss

It is common for people in forensic situations, such as criminal defense, personal injury lawsuits, and disability cases, to claim memory loss, poor concentration, and lessened intellectual abilities. Some individuals may argue that their memory problems make it difficult for them to remember important events, follow the trial, or manage independently. Although conditions such as traumatic brain injury, dementia, or neurodevelopmental disorders are real, some people may pretend to have them to avoid responsibilities or get what they want.

Often, the symptoms of malingered cognitive impairment are either very severe or do not match the person's actual behavior. People might say they cannot remember a particular event, but they often recall many details about something else. Some people may not perform well on simple memory tests, yet they can recall and use information when speaking. A few individuals may exaggerate their difficulties, saying they cannot read or write, but they can do these tasks in other situations.

In such situations, it is crucial to utilize formal performance validity testing. The Test of Memory Malingering (TOMM), Word

Memory Test (WMT), and Rey 15-Item Test are used to assess the effort and consistency a person exhibits in their cognitive tasks. The purpose of these tests is to find out if someone's performance is lower than it should be, even in those with real cognitive problems. If a person fails on several validity measures, it is likely they are malingering, and their symptoms should not be trusted.

The psychiatrist should check the patient's medical and school records to understand their normal functioning. When severe cognitive problems appear suddenly, and there is no known injury, neurological event, or previous impairment, it is suspicious. In some cases, reports from family, friends, or supervisors can reveal discrepancies between the person's reported problems and their actual daily activities.

Psychotic Disorders

Another issue in forensic psychiatry is when a person pretends to have psychosis during criminal responsibility evaluations. As Kushwaha et al. (2024) explained, people accused of serious crimes may pretend to have hallucinations or delusions or behave in a disorganized way to try and be considered legally insane at the time of the offense. Because psychosis is widely misunderstood and carries much stigma, it is often targeted by people who fake mental illness.

People malingering with psychosis tend to show unusual or exaggerated symptoms that are not typical of psychosis. For instance, some people may report hearing voices that are always too loud, never going away, and always giving orders without any disagreement. Unlike theatrical voices, genuine auditory hallucinations tend to be irregular, confusing, and upsetting rather than just strange. Likewise, malingered delusions may not make sense, change often, and lack the order and consistency found in real psychosis.

It is important to observe behavior in various environments. Kushwaha et al. (2024) explain that individuals who exhibit psychopathic behavior in the doctor's office but act normally when they believe no one is watching may be engaging in pretense. Other signs may include sudden changes in mood, using medical terms to describe symptoms, or experiencing intense outbursts that seem unprovoked. The MMPI-2/MMPI-3 (Minnesota Multiphasic Personality Inventory) is a formal test that can show if a person's answers about psychotic symptoms are exaggerated or inconsistent.

Mood Disorders

People may pretend to have depression, mania, or suicidal thoughts in order to avoid being tried or sent to prison. Some people may pretend to feel extremely sad, hopeless, or suicidal to seem unwell or in crisis. Even though depression and mood disorders are common and severe, their symptoms can be misunderstood, mainly when there are obvious external rewards.

Signs of malingered mood disorders are extreme or constant reporting of symptoms, differences between a person's reported mood and their actual behavior, and the absence of related symptoms such as trouble sleeping, eating, or focusing. Someone who says they are too depressed to leave bed might also describe themselves as being very awake and full of energy during the interview. A person who talks about suicide but does not appear upset or urgent may not be taken seriously.

The Beck Depression Inventory-II (BDI-II), along with validity indicators, can be used to differentiate depression from overstated symptoms. While reviewing cases related to mood, a forensic psychiatrist should consider how symptoms have developed over the years, how the person was handled in the past and if these symptoms influence daily life.

10.3 Ethical Reporting of Suspected Malingering

It is necessary to be objective, relevant to the law and responsible when reporting malingering in forensic psychiatry. Walczyk et al. (2018) mention that accusing someone of deception in mental health can result in major consequences. It can change peoples' legal rights, the way others view them, whether they get help and their access to medical care. For this reason, forensic psychiatrists ought to be precise, accurate and based on evidence in everything they write or say. They should stay neutral, not let their own opinions affect their work and use trustworthy information when making statements.

Malingering is not a mental illness; it is just a way to get something from outside sources. Unlike factitious disorder or somatic symptom disorder, this condition is not caused by a person's inner psychological needs. Psychiatrists should not decide that someone is malingering unless they are sure of the person's intentions. The label can be seen as stigmatizing and could be opposed in court or by experts who disagree. For this reason, every report should include documented inconsistencies, confirmed assessment findings, and a clear explanation of the reasoning process.

Forensic psychiatrists should first explain the referral question and the setting of the evaluation when reporting suspected malingering. The report could explain that the person was referred to evaluate their responsibility for the crime, their ability to participate in a trial, or their disability. Walczyk et al. (2018) explain that this contextual approach explains the use of effort testing, behavioral observation, and validity scales. It also indicates that the evaluator is not responsible for treatment but for answering legal questions using clinical evidence.

The findings should be presented without bias and based solely on facts. The report should include people's descriptions of the symptoms, their medical background, the results of tests, and how the behavior is related. Rix and Tracy (2018) suggest that any unusual behaviors should be explained with specific examples. For example, the psychiatrist could find that the individuals reported hearing voices all the time. However, they were not distracted; they answered questions logically and were seen laughing and interacting with others in other places. The report may also mention that the patient's symptoms did not match typical patterns or that their performance on effort tests was far below what would be expected by chance, using references to standard data.

When discussing suspected malingering, language is critical. Avoiding words that could be perceived as accusatory or inflammatory helps maintain a professional and objective tone. It is better to say that the results indicate feigned symptoms or that the person did not perform credibly on validity tests rather than calling them a malingerer. This approach enables evaluators to exercise their clinical judgment without explicitly stating the motivation or intent of the person (Rix& Tracy, 2018). Suppose the evidence is strong but uncertain. In that case, the psychiatrist may say, "It is possible that the patient is malingering" or "The results suggest the patient may be exaggerating or lying."

Ethical rules also stress the need for proportionality. If the suspicion of malingering arises from just one small detail, it may not be justified to make significant assumptions. The diagnosis should only be used when there is agreement among several sources; for example, when someone's behavior differs from what they say, their test scores are poor on multiple measures, and there is no supporting evidence. Even so, the conclusion should focus on the effects on society and the law rather than on what is right or wrong.

Forensic psychiatrists must consider the implications of their findings. If malingering is found, it can result in a person being sent to prison, denied disability support, or refused mental health care. Sometimes, if the deception is considered fraudulent, it may lead to criminal charges (Rix& Tracy, 2018). As a result, it is essential to be cautious at every stage of the evaluation, from data collection to documentation. The psychiatrist should not investigate or enforce but instead offer an expert opinion based on clinical and ethical principles.

Handling confidentiality is very important. In forensic cases, the person being evaluated is typically aware that the results will be sent to the court or referring agency. Still, the report should contain only details that pertain to the legal question. Avoid including personal information that is not relevant, speculation, or language that is emotionally charged. The report needs to be structured, easy to understand, and focused, and it should include a summary of the findings and a well-reasoned conclusion.

If the evidence for malingering is inconclusive, it may be advisable to suggest additional testing or ongoing observation. If a person displays some signs of exaggeration, describes distressing symptoms, and has a background in psychiatric treatment, the psychiatrist may advise observing the individual in a controlled environment (Rix& Tracy, 2018). By following this approach, psychiatrists avoid making unfair judgments about a person based on limited information.

It is also important to work with legal professionals. Forensic psychiatrists are expected to explain their findings in court, answer questions from attorneys or judges, and explain what their evaluation does not cover. This means describing how malingering is evaluated, the tools used, and the reasons behind the important findings. Being open and transparent helps establish trust in the psychiatrist's opinion and supports the court's decision-making process.

Ethics also influence the way suspected malingering is addressed in meetings with different professionals. During team meetings, consultations, or when writing professional reports, the psychiatrist should refrain from making negative or disrespectful comments. The purpose is to supply correct information to guide the best legal or medical decision, not to shame or punish the individual. Sometimes, malingering people may also be dealing with psychological issues such as personality disorders, past trauma, or lack of social support. Even though these do not excuse lying, they can help explain someone's actions and guide future actions.

10.4 Summary and Takeaways

Malingering is a significant problem in forensic psychiatry because it is done deliberately, and the outcomes can be critical in legal cases. Malingering is different from real mental illness because it involves intentionally making or exaggerating symptoms to benefit oneself. Forensic psychiatrists should utilize their training, interviews, tests, and observations to assess the reliability of the reported symptoms. To identify inconsistencies and check efforts, clinicians rely on the SIRS, MMPI, and TOMM tests.

PTSD, cognitive deficits, psychosis, and depression are among the disorders that are more likely to be faked. Such presentations may include unusual signs that do not usually occur in ordinary illnesses, for example, very strong or dramatic symptoms or those that seem unpredictable. It is important for psychiatrists to know what the common symptoms are and what limitations exist when using various tools for diagnosis.

Any suspicion of malingering calls for and requires proper reporting by a psychiatrist. They ought to be sincere and clear and substantiate what they find in their explanations. It is important to think about suspicion of malingering when there are various similar signs and the choice should be based on both medical and legal points. This work centers on preventing anything harmful, remaining impartial and making everything just. If forensic psychiatrists follow good evaluation methods and ethical guidelines, they can decide whether a patient's symptoms are true or made up.

Chapter 11: Conducting Forensic Evaluations

Forensic evaluations are a key part of forensic psychiatrists' work. They help courts and legal authorities by providing expert opinions on a person's mental state and ability to decide or take risks. According to Chadda (2013), unlike clinical assessments, forensic evaluations are conducted for legal reasons and require the evaluator to be objective, clear, and ethical. These evaluations involve complex cases where mental health and legal matters, such as criminal responsibility, fitness to trial, civil capacity or risk to others, are intertwined. A proper forensic evaluation involves a step-by-step process that includes interviewing the subject, studying additional data and applying the proper legal rules. Forensic psychiatrists have to deal with issues such as bias, role confusion, and effectively sharing their results with legal professionals. This chapter discusses the main steps of conducting a forensic evaluation, which include planning, interviewing, documenting, and communicating. It also provides practical templates for handling various kinds of forensic assessments.

11.1 Principles of Forensic Interviewing

Forensic interviewing differs from clinical interviewing in both its goals and approach. Faller (2021) explains that clinical interviews are meant to diagnose and treat, but forensic interviews are used to answer legal questions. The interviews should be fair, complete and ethical, with the forensic psychiatrist acting as an evaluator for the court, not as a caregiver.

The first principle of forensic interviewing is clarity of purpose. The psychiatrist must know the exact legal question that the referral seeks to answer. Whether the assessment is for criminal responsibility, fitness to stand trial or civil capacity, the interview must remain focused on gathering information relevant to that issue. It helps avoid collecting unnecessary data and prevents the interview from drifting into a therapeutic mode.

Establishing boundaries at the beginning of the interview is crucial. The psychiatrist must inform the individual that the evaluation is not for treatment but for legal purposes. This disclosure should include information about who will receive the report, how the information will be used, and the limits of confidentiality (Faller, 2021). Explaining these facts in clear and straightforward language helps avoid misunderstandings and protects the evaluator from ethical concerns later.

Another core element is neutrality. Unlike therapists, forensic psychiatrists must remain impartial and avoid aligning with the individual being evaluated. Empathy may still be appropriate; especially to build rapport, but it should never compromise objectivity (Faller, 2021). The psychiatrist must resist any urge to advocate for or against the person and instead rely on evidence, structured tools, and professional judgment to support their conclusions.

Interview structure is important for ensuring consistency and thoroughness. Forensic interviews typically begin with open-ended questions, allowing the persons to describe their experiences, followed by more specific probes to clarify timelines, symptoms, and behaviors. According to Bernath (2021), this technique allows the psychiatrist to observe the person's narrative style, thought process, and ability to respond without suggestion. It also helps identify any inconsistencies or signs of malingering.

The content of the interview depends on the evaluation type but often includes psychiatric history, medical history, developmental background, educational and occupational functioning, legal history, and substance use. For criminal evaluations, details about the offense are also essential. The psychiatrist must understand the person's mental state at the time of the alleged offense or at the time of the evaluation, depending on the applicable legal standard.

Behavioral observations play a vital role in forensic interviews. The psychiatrist should note how the person presents, speaks, and interacts. Do they make eye contact? Do their verbal and non-verbal expressions match? Are there signs of exaggeration or minimization? These observations can help verify or challenge the consistency of reported symptoms. They are instrumental when assessing conditions such as psychosis, mood disorders, or malingering.

Cultural competence is another critical factor. The psychiatrist must remain aware of how individuals' cultural background, language, and social norms might influence their behavior, beliefs, and symptom expression. Failure to consider these factors may lead to incorrect conclusions or biased interpretations (Bernath, 2021). In forensic settings, where evaluations may significantly impact a person's liberty or legal outcome, such misjudgments can be especially harmful.

Managing resistance is common in forensic interviews. Individuals may be uncooperative, angry, confused, or manipulative. The psychiatrist must remain calm, professional, and persistent without being confrontational. If the individual refuses to participate, partial assessments can still be conducted using collateral information (Bernath, 2021). A respectful but firm approach can encourage engagement, even when initial resistance is high.

Note-taking and documentation during the interview should be thorough and accurate. It is helpful to document direct quotes, especially when they are unusual, contradictory, or legally significant. While audio or video recording may be used in some jurisdictions, written notes remain essential and should include observations, content, and the evaluator's impressions.

Avoiding suggestive questioning is essential. Leading questions can distort the individual's responses or create false impressions. The psychiatrist should allow the persons to describe symptoms in their own words before asking, clarifying, or confirming questions. It is essential in assessments of psychosis, trauma, or memory-related issues.

Finally, forensic interviewing requires patience and flexibility. Some evaluations take more than one session, particularly when the person is anxious, disorganized, or defensive. The psychiatrists must be prepared to adjust their approach based on the person's condition and the pace at which they can provide reliable information.

11.2 Gathering Collateral Information

In forensic psychiatry, gathering collateral information is just as important as interviewing with the individual. While self-reports provide valuable insights, they may be biased, incomplete, or inaccurate, especially in legal settings. Owoyemi et al. (2021) state that people under evaluation may withhold details, exaggerate symptoms, or distort facts for various reasons. Therefore, reviewing collateral information allows forensic psychiatrists to verify claims, understand the broader context, and reach well-informed conclusions.

Collateral sources include a wide range of records and accounts. These may involve medical and psychiatric histories, school records, employment files, police reports, court documents, correctional records, social services files, and previous evaluations (Owoyemi et al., 2021). Witness statements and interviews with family members, caregivers, or legal representatives can also provide helpful context. Each of these sources adds another layer of understanding, thereby strengthening the credibility of the forensic opinion.

The first step in using collateral information is obtaining proper consent or legal authorization. If the individual is not the one requesting the evaluation, the referring agency often holds the authority to release records. However, forensic psychiatrists must still adhere to privacy laws and professional ethics (Owoyemi et al., 2021). They must only protect sensitive data from unauthorized disclosure and access and disclose information that is necessary for addressing the specific legal question.

Reviewing records should begin with identifying timelines and discrepancies. The psychiatrist should compare statements made during the interview with those found in prior reports (Petrik et al., 2015). For example, if people claim to have never had mental health treatment but hospital discharge summaries show multiple admissions; this may raise questions about credibility or insight. Conversely, if their narrative aligns with documented facts, it lends weight to their account.

Police and court records are invaluable in criminal evaluations. They provide detailed accounts of the offense, witness testimony, and judicial findings. These records can help clarify what happened, when it occurred, and how the person behaved before, during, and after the incident. Such information is critical in assessing the mental state at the time of the offense or the person's fitness to stand trial.

Medical and psychiatric records offer insight into diagnosis, treatment history, medication compliance, and previous risk behaviors. They also show how the individual has responded to past interventions. A long history of noncompliance or repeated hospitalizations may indicate chronic instability (Petrik et al., 2015). On the other hand, steady progress in outpatient settings may indicate improved functioning and lower risk.

Educational records are often important in evaluations involving juveniles or those with intellectual disabilities. They help assess developmental milestones, behavioral issues, and academic achievement.

These factors are particularly relevant when evaluating cognitive capacity, social maturity, and the presence of neurodevelopmental conditions. In civil matters, such as guardianship or testamentary capacity evaluations, employment records and financial documents may show how the person has managed responsibilities, made decisions, and handled stress (Petrik et al., 2015). These patterns offer indirect evidence about cognitive functioning and adaptive behavior.

Witnesses and collateral interviews must be approached carefully. Family members, friends, or employers can offer unique perspectives, but their accounts may also be biased. Yohananoff (2016) states that the forensic psychiatrist must evaluate the reliability and potential motives of each informant. For instance, a parent involved in a custody battle may downplay or exaggerate the other parent's mental state. Still, such input may be helpful when interpreted in light of other evidence.

In some cases, especially those involving memory concerns or alleged trauma, psychological testing can be used to cross-check claims. When records and self-reports diverge, these tests can help clarify functioning, symptom severity, and effort (Yohananoff, 2016). However, they must be interpreted by professionals trained in psychological assessment and understood as one part of the larger evaluation.

Forensic psychiatrists must always document how collateral information influences their opinion. Reports should include summaries of key documents and clearly explain how those records support or challenge the conclusions drawn from them. This transparency helps courts understand the evaluator's reasoning and assess the credibility of the findings.

11.3 Avoiding Common Pitfalls: Bias, Dual Roles, and Ethical Hazards

Forensic evaluations demand a high standard of objectivity and professional integrity. According to Pedersen et al. (2025), forensic psychiatrists must be aware of several common pitfalls that can compromise the validity of an evaluation, including bias, role confusion, and ethical oversights. Avoiding these issues is essential to produce fair, defensible, and ethically sound reports.

Bias can take many forms, whether people are aware of it or not, and it can influence how the evaluator interprets the data, perceives the person, or draws a conclusion. Psychiatrists may give more attention to facts that support their initial impression and overlook those that contradict it. As Pedersen et al. (2025) explain, this happens when evaluators decide on a hypothesis early and use it to interpret all the findings. Forensic psychiatrists should regularly reevaluate their beliefs and seek evidence that might challenge their theories to minimize the risk of error.

Another form of bias is adversarial allegiance. It happens when evaluators have a gentle agreement with the person who hired them, such as a defence attorney or a prosecuting agency. Even if they have good intentions, professionals should give an opinion that aligns with that of the referral source (Pedersen et al., 2025). The evaluation should be fair and rely only on facts, regardless of who requested it.

Cultural bias also poses a challenge. Evaluators must remain sensitive to cultural differences in communication, values, and behavior. Misinterpreting culturally normative behavior as pathology or missing key contextual details may result in flawed assessments (Pedersen et al., 2025). Training in cultural competence and awareness of one's assumptions helps mitigate this form of error.

Role confusion is another serious concern. A forensic psychiatrist must clearly distinguish the evaluator role from that of a treating clinician. These roles have fundamentally different goals: therapy is aimed at healing, while forensic evaluations focus on providing information to legal systems. Mixing these roles can create ethical problems and damage the credibility of the report.

For example, treating psychiatrists who are asked to write forensic reports on their patients may struggle to maintain objectivity. According to Gordon (2016), their therapeutic relationship might bias their opinion, and their dual role may violate patient trust. Similarly, an evaluator must not begin therapy with someone they have assessed for legal purposes, as this reverses the ethical flow and may confuse the patient about the nature of the relationship.

In correctional and institutional settings, dual roles can arise when forensic psychiatrists conduct risk assessments on individuals they have clinically monitored. According to Gordon (2016), institutions may expect them to act as both care providers and evaluators; however, clear boundaries must be established to prevent ethical conflicts. It may be appropriate to decline one role or recommend that another professional take over to maintain clarity and impartiality.

Informed consent is another area where forensic psychiatrists must exercise particular care and caution. Unlike clinical practice, where patients voluntarily seek care, individuals in forensic evaluations may not fully understand their rights or the purpose of the interview. According to Gordon (2016), evaluators must explain that the assessment is not confidential in the usual clinical sense and that the results will be shared with legal or administrative authorities. Consent should include a clear explanation of what the evaluation involves, how the findings will be used, and any limits to privacy. Failure to provide this information undermines ethical practice and can invalidate the assessment.

Documentation and transparency are essential safeguards against ethical concerns. According to Gordon (2016), forensic psychiatrists should keep detailed notes of interviews, document their rationale for conclusions, and clearly explain how each piece of information contributed to their opinion. This practice safeguards against accusations of bias or incompetence, ensuring that others can review and understand the process.

Forensic evaluators must also avoid advocacy. Their role is not to promote the interests of one party but to provide objective findings to inform a legal decision. Becoming emotionally involved in a case, overidentifying with an individual, or attempting to influence the legal outcome exceeds the proper scope of forensic practice.

Lastly, time pressure and workload can lead to shortcuts that compromise quality. Skipping collateral information, rushing interviews, or recycling text from prior reports may seem efficient, but they compromise the evaluation's uniqueness and credibility. Forensic psychiatry requires methodical and careful work, even under challenging conditions.

11.4 Structuring a Forensic Report: Dos and Don'ts

The forensic report is the final and most visible product of a forensic evaluation. It communicates findings, clinical impressions, and professional opinions to courts, lawyers, and other decision-makers. According to Brannick (2015), a well-structured report demonstrates competence, objectivity, and respect for both legal and psychiatric standards. It should be clear, concise, organized, and tailored to its legal purpose.

A good report begins with a clear identification section. It includes the name of the individual, date of birth, case number, referral source, date of the evaluation, and the name of the forensic psychiatrist. According to Brannick (2015), the opening should clearly state who requested the review and for what purpose, such as an assessment of fitness to stand trial, criminal responsibility, or risk. Clearly stating the purpose at the outset helps readers understand the relevance of the findings.

Next, the evaluator should summarize the sources of information used. It includes interviews with the individual, collateral interviews with family or staff, medical records, legal documents, police reports, psychological testing, and observations (Brannick, 2015). Listing all data sources shows the thoroughness of the process and enhances credibility. If any key source was unavailable, the report should note this and describe how it may limit the validity of the opinion.

The background or psychosocial history section follows. This section should present a narrative of the person's life, including early development, education, family background, employment history, substance use, legal history, and medical and psychiatric history. The goal is to paint a comprehensive picture of the person's functioning over time. However, the report must avoid unnecessary detail and focus on information relevant to the legal question.

The mental status examination (MSE) provides a quick overview of the person's current mental state. Milton (2020) explains that it consists of appearance, behavior and mood, speech, thought processes, perceptions, cognition, and insight. The MSE should be written in a factual and unbiased manner, mentioning any unusual findings neutrally and objectively. If the MSE does not match what was previously observed or recorded, the report must explain the discrepancy.

The findings from testing should always be well explained. Milton (2020) states that the report should outline the tests administered, the outcomes, and how they are clinically significant. If the person took a test for malingering or cognitive abilities, the results should be considered in conjunction with all other information in the case. The findings from psychometric tests should be explained in simple terms, but the reasoning behind them should be easy to follow.

The opinion section is the most critical part of the report. It must directly answer the legal question. For example, in a fitness-to-stand trial evaluation, the report must state whether the individual understands court proceedings and is capable of assisting counsel. According to Tejani (2022), the opinion should be written in plain language and supported by clear reasoning. Avoiding vague or overly technical statements makes the report more useful to legal professionals.

Importantly, evaluators should explain how they arrived at their conclusions. It includes connecting the data from interviews, testing, and collateral sources to the legal criteria. According to Tejani (2022), each element of the legal standard should be addressed separately. For example, in a criminal responsibility report, the evaluator should consider whether a mental illness was present at the time of the offense and, if so, whether it affected the individual's ability to understand the nature of the act or its wrongfulness.

The tone of the report must remain neutral and respectful. Derogatory or judgmental language should be avoided. The focus should be on behavior, not moral character. Forensic psychiatrists must write with the understanding that their reports may be read by judges, attorneys, and even the individuals being evaluated.

There are several common pitfalls to avoid in report writing. They include the following:

Using vague language. Terms like "appears" or "possibly" should be used cautiously and explained.

Overstating certainty. Forensic psychiatry is not an exact science. Statements should reflect the level of confidence in the opinion.

Copying text from templates or prior reports. While templates are helpful, reports must be personalized to the case. Reused content can suggest carelessness.

Omitting key limitations. If there were barriers to a complete assessment, such as incomplete records or uncooperative behavior, this should be disclosed.

Failing to distinguish facts from interpretation. Reports should separate observed behavior from the evaluator's analysis.

Each report should conclude with a signed declaration stating that the opinions are based on the evaluator's professional expertise, that no party has influenced them, and that the report is accurate to the best of their knowledge. Including this statement helps affirm the ethical and professional integrity of the evaluation. A forensic report is both a clinical and legal document. It must meet high standards of clarity, relevance, and objectivity. With careful structure and attention to detail, forensic psychiatrists can produce reports that meaningfully assist courts in making informed decisions.

11.5 Communicating Findings to Legal Professionals

Writing a clear and well-supported forensic report is only part of the task. According to Koch (2025), forensic psychiatrists must also be able to communicate their findings effectively to legal professionals, both in writing and in person. It includes preparing for court testimony, responding to legal questions, and explaining psychiatric concepts in a manner that is understandable to lawyers and judges.

Unlike clinical reports, forensic evaluations are meant to inform a legal decision. It means that how the findings are presented can influence outcomes such as sentencing, treatment mandates, or even acquittal. According to Koch (2025), communication should be accurate, objective, and free from medical jargon. The language should be neutral and professional, avoiding speculative or emotionally charged terms.

When preparing to communicate findings, the psychiatrist should first be clear on the legal standard being addressed. Legal professionals rely on these evaluations to answer specific questions, such as whether an individual meets the criteria for Fitness to Stand Trial or whether a mental disorder influences their criminal behavior (Koch, 2025). Therefore, all communications should begin by restating the legal question and directly tying the opinion to that standard.

In court settings, forensic psychiatrists often provide expert testimony. It may occur during hearings on fitness, responsibility, civil commitment, or risk. According to Van Es et al. (2020), during testimony, psychiatrists should remain calm, factual, and concise in their responses. The goal is to educate the court- not advocate for one side. Psychiatrists are not lawyers, and their job is not to argue a case but to offer an impartial professional opinion.

Legal professionals may ask complex or even confrontational questions. According to Van Es et al. (2020), forensic psychiatrists should listen carefully, take their time responding, and clarify any misinterpretations that may arise. If they do not know the answer, it is appropriate to say so rather than speculate. Admitting the limits of one's knowledge can enhance credibility and show respect for the court process.

In written communications, it is helpful to use clear headings, bullet points, and structured sections. It allows legal professionals to navigate the document easily and identify key findings. According to Van Es et al. (2020), psychiatrists should avoid using long, dense paragraphs or excessive technical language. When technical terms are necessary, define them. For instance, if referring to a diagnosis of schizophrenia, briefly explain its symptoms and relevance to the legal issue.

Visual aids can be helpful in some situations. Charts, timelines, or summaries of test scores may clarify complex information. However, visual material should always be simple and professionally formatted. The goal is not to impress but to inform.

Another important aspect of communication is transparency. According to Golumbeck (2013), psychiatrists should explain not only their conclusions but also the reasoning behind them. It includes discussing which data was most influential, acknowledging any contradictory information, and describing how uncertainty was handled. For instance, if the opinion is that someone is fit to stand Trial despite moderate cognitive impairment, the psychiatrist should explain how the individual compensates and how that affects their legal capacities.

Psychiatrists should also be prepared to respond to cross-examination. This may involve defending their methodology, the tools they used, or their interpretation of findings. Familiarity with one's report, test data, and key sources is essential. Anticipating possible challenges and preparing clear, respectful answers helps maintain composure under pressure.

Sometimes, legal professionals request clarification after receiving the report. Forensic psychiatrists should respond promptly and in writing, always keeping a copy for their records. Any supplementary opinions or corrections should be documented carefully and clearly labeled as such.

In rare cases, courts may ask for oral reports or summaries. These situations require careful preparation. Golumbeck (2013) states that the psychiatrist should prepare brief talking points that summarize the opinion, key data, and conclusions. Legal professionals often appreciate concise summaries that they can refer to during proceedings.

Finally, communication must respect ethical boundaries. Forensic psychiatrists should never promise a particular outcome, advocate for one side, or alter findings under pressure. All communications must reflect the psychiatrist's independent professional judgment. This commitment to objectivity is what gives forensic psychiatric opinions their value in court.

11.6 Sample Templates for Common Evaluations (for example, FST, CR)

Forensic psychiatrists frequently perform standardized evaluations that must meet legal standards while also reflecting psychiatric rigor. Two of the most common assessments are Fitness to Stand Trial (FST) and Criminal Responsibility (CR). Using structured templates helps ensure consistency, clarity, and legal relevance. The templates below offer a general guide for how such evaluations may be organized.

A. Fitness to Stand Trial (FST) Template

Referral and legal context. Begin with a brief explanation of the referral source, the purpose of the evaluation, and legal criteria for determining fitness in the relevant jurisdiction. State the date of the request and any deadlines.

Example:"This report was prepared at the request of the court to evaluate Mr. X's current fitness to stand trial under [name of legal standard]. The legal issue concerns whether the defendant possesses sufficient mental capacity to understand the proceedings and assist in his defense."

Sources of information. List all materials reviewed: interviews, medical records, legal documents, psychological testing, and collateral sources.

Interview summary. Describe the interview setting, duration, rapport, and behavior during the assessment. Include any relevant disclosures or unusual behavior.

Mental status examination. Include appearance, behavior and mood, thought process, perception, cognition, insight, and judgment.

Legal abilities evaluation. Address the core legal competencies:

- Do the individuals understand the charges?
- Can they understand the roles of court personnel?
- Do they grasp the nature of the legal process?
- Can they assist counsel rationally?
- Can they make decisions in their best interest?

Include examples and observations supporting each answer.

Psychiatric diagnosis. Summarize any mental disorder or condition that may impair legal functioning.

Opinion. Provide a clear, concise statement of whether the individual is fit to stand trial based on the evidence.

Example: "Based on the available information, Mr. X currently demonstrates sufficient understanding of legal proceedings and can assist his attorney. He is therefore considered fit to stand trial."

Recommendations. If the individual is unfit, provide suggestions for restoration, such as inpatient treatment or education about legal procedures.

B. Criminal Responsibility (CR) Template

Referral and legal context. State who referred the case and define the legal standard for criminal responsibility in a specific jurisdiction (for instance, M'Naghten Rule, ALI standard).

Example: "This evaluation was requested to determine whether Mr. Y was legally responsible for his actions at the time of the alleged offense under the [name of legal standard]."

Sources of information. List police reports, witness statements, video footage, medical and psychiatric history, and collateral interviews.

Description of the offense. Summarize the nature of the alleged crime based on available evidence. Include the date, location, and the individual's behavior before, during, and after the offense.

Mental state at the time of the offense. Present psychiatric findings relevant to the individual's mental state during the event. Consider delusions, hallucinations, mood episodes, disorganized thoughts, or intoxication. Include statements from the accused and others.

Psychiatric diagnosis. List all current and relevant past diagnoses, noting if they were active at the time of the offense.

Functional impact. Explain whether the mental disorder affected the individuals' abilities to:

- Understand the wrongfulness of their actions.
- Conform their behavior to the law.
- Act with intent or premeditation.

Opinion. Clearly state whether the individual meets the legal standard for lack of criminal responsibility.

Example: "At the time of the offense, Mr. Y was suffering from a severe psychotic disorder. He was unable to appreciate the wrongfulness of his actions and is therefore considered not criminally responsible."

Recommendations. Suggest appropriate next steps: diversion to psychiatric care, treatment in a secure hospital, or risk assessments.

11.7 Summary and Takeaways

Conducting forensic evaluations requires a balance of clinical expertise, legal knowledge, and clear communication. Forensic psychiatrists play a critical role in answering specific legal questions, such as Fitness to Stand Trial and Criminal Responsibility. Effective evaluations depend on thorough interviews, collateral information, and careful use of structured tools. Bias, dual roles, and unclear reasoning can undermine the credibility of a report and the fairness of legal proceedings.

Well-structured forensic reports adhere to a consistent format, remain focused on the legal issue, and clearly explain the basis for each opinion. They must be written in plain, accessible language for legal professionals. Testimony and communication skills are equally important, especially in adversarial legal settings. Forensic psychiatrists must stay neutral, speak clearly, and prepare for cross-examination with calm professionalism.

Using templates helps ensure that all critical points are included in every evaluation. Yet, each report should highlight what makes the case unique. When assessments in forensic psychiatry are conducted ethically, precisely, and based on evidence, they significantly aid justice. Using their clinical and legal knowledge, forensic psychiatrists assist courts in making just and fair decisions about people with mental disorders in the legal system.

Chapter 12: Testifying in Court

Forensic psychiatrists find testifying in court to be one of the most challenging aspects of their job. It involves possessing medical knowledge, understanding the law, ability to communicate well, and being emotionally resilient. Van Es et al. (2020) point out that while preparing reports is a private task, testifying means the psychiatrist's work is open to public view, challenging questions, and possible criticism from other experts and lawyers. Forensic psychiatrists offer objective advice to the court, not to support any particular party. They should be honest about their findings, make complex psychiatric matters understandable, and act professionally at all times during the legal process. This chapter demonstrates how to present testimony effectively in court. It explains how forensic psychiatrists should prepare for depositions and cross-examinations; interact well with judges and juries, identify and address biases, and handle challenging legal cases. When they master these skills, forensic psychiatrists help ensure fairness in the law and preserve their professional standards.

12.1 Preparing for Depositions and Cross-Examination

When forensic psychiatrists appear in court, they must go beyond their clinical knowledge. One of the most challenging aspects of this job is going through depositions and being questioned by opposing counsel. Heilbrun (2006) points out that, unlike in a clinic, where people work together and support each other, in a courtroom, everything said can be closely examined and challenged. In this context, preparation becomes the cornerstone of an effective testimony. Without adequate preparation, even the most knowledgeable and experienced forensic psychiatrist may struggle to present their opinions clearly and withstand the pressures of adversarial questioning.

Preparation for testimony begins long before entering the courtroom or deposition room. The forensic psychiatrist must first possess a thorough understanding of the legal question at issue. In every case, whether the evaluation concerns criminal responsibility, fitness to stand trial, testamentary capacity, or civil commitment, the expert must be fully aware of the specific legal standard being applied. According to Heilbrun (2006), the psychiatrist's role is not to offer general psychiatric opinions but to address the legal criteria directly. Reviewing the legal statutes, case law, and jurisdictional guidelines that govern the evaluation ensures that the expert remains within the appropriate scope of their testimony.

Central to preparation is the comprehensive review of all case materials. According to Grisso (2006), forensic psychiatrists must reacquaint themselves with the entirety of the evaluation file, including their report, interview notes, collateral information, psychological testing results, and any supplementary records obtained since the initial assessment. Often, considerable time passes between the evaluation and the date of testimony, making this review essential. Without a fresh and detailed understanding of the case, the psychiatrist risks being unprepared for the nuanced questions that may arise.

Equally important is the ability to critically review one's report with an unbiased and self-analytical perspective. This action requires psychiatrists to read their work not simply as the authors but as opposing attorneys might read it, with the intent of identifying inconsistencies, weaknesses, or gaps in reasoning. Certain sections may be open to different interpretations or raise questions that were not fully addressed. According to Grisso (2006), anticipating these challenges allows the psychiatrist to develop clear, reasoned explanations that can withstand adversarial questioning. A well-prepared expert must not only know their conclusions but also be able to explain why and how those conclusions were reached, even when challenged.

It is essential to practice and expect the questions that may be asked during cross-examination. Experienced lawyers may try to weaken the expert's testimony by using a few common tactics. They may point out minor mistakes in the report, suggest that some key information was overlooked, question the evaluator's skills, or propose alternative ways to understand the evidence. According to Gold and Frierson (2017), forensic psychiatrists should be ready for these challenges and plan out their responses in advance. A good way to get prepared is to participate in mock cross-examinations. Practicing being questioned by an attorney allows the psychiatrists to remain calm and focused, thereby improving their ability to respond clearly without being defensive.

Besides being knowledgeable about the facts, the expert should be ready to explain the science behind their findings. Gold and Frierson (2017) state that forensic psychiatrists should consult the psychiatric literature to support their opinions, especially any relevant studies, guidelines, or professional standards mentioned in the report. It is not uncommon for opposing counsel to question the foundation of an expert's conclusions by challenging their understanding of current research. The psychiatrist should be able to cite authoritative sources and explain how the scientific evidence supports their findings while remaining within the limits of broadly accepted psychiatric knowledge.

Preparation for deposition testimony deserves particular attention. Depositions are sworn statements taken outside of court, often with attorneys present but without a judge or jury. According to Gold and Frierson (2017), while the environment may seem less formal, depositions are legally binding and may be used to impeach the psychiatrist's credibility during later court proceedings. Any inconsistencies between deposition testimony and in-court statements can seriously damage the psychiatrist's credibility. Therefore, depositions require the same level of preparation, care, and professionalism as live testimony in a courtroom.

In addition to content preparation, the psychiatrist must engage in psychological preparation for the demands of adversarial questioning. Attorneys may employ tactics designed not only to challenge the psychiatrist's opinions but also to provoke frustration, confusion, or emotional reactions. The ability to remain composed, listen carefully, and respond only to the specific question being asked is a skill that requires conscious practice. According to Heilbrun (2006), forensic psychiatrists must train themselves to pause before answering, resist the temptation to volunteer unnecessary information and maintain a steady, respectful tone even when questions seem unfair or confrontational.

One crucial communication strategy is to answer questions directly and succinctly. Rambling answers may provide opposing counsel with opportunities to introduce new lines of questioning. Instead, the psychiatrist should respond only to the question posed, providing brief, factual answers unless further elaboration is necessary for accuracy and clarity. According to Doak et al. (2021), if a question is unclear or misleading, the psychiatrist should request clarification before responding to it. An expert who is well-prepared stays focused on the facts and does not let themselves be guided by guesses or unsupported ideas.

In addition, familiarity with courtroom procedures enhances the psychiatrist's confidence and professionalism when testifying. It means knowing the order of direct and cross-examination, where to sit, how to address the judge, and how to follow courtroom etiquette. Even the most minor details, such as wearing the right attire, speaking clearly, and maintaining eye contact with the judge or jury, can help the expert appear more credible and effective.

Preparation for depositions and cross-examinations is a multifaceted process that extends beyond mere knowledge of the facts. It requires mastery of the case material, a clear understanding of legal standards, critical self-review, anticipation of opposing strategies, and disciplined communication under pressure. The forensic psychiatrist who approaches testimony with thorough preparation and professional composure becomes a valuable asset to the court, offering reliable, transparent, and impartial expert opinions even in the most challenging legal settings.

12.2 Effective Communication with Judges and Juries

Forensic psychiatrists serve a unique role in courtrooms, bridging the gap between the specialized language of psychiatry and the legal system's need for understandable, practical information. Wathen (2005) states that unlike clinical practice, where the psychiatrist communicates primarily with fellow medical professionals, court testimony requires the expert to explain complex psychiatric concepts to judges and juries who often have little or no background in mental health. Effective communication with these legal audiences is crucial for ensuring that the psychiatrist's opinions are accurately understood, properly evaluated, and fairly applied in legal decisions.

The first challenge in communicating with judges and juries is recognizing the significant difference in professional language. Psychiatry relies on specialized terminology to describe mental states, behaviors, and diagnoses. Terms such as "thought disorganization," "anosognosia," or "executive dysfunction" may be second nature in clinical discussions, but they hold little meaning for legal audiences without clear explanation. According to Otto et al. (2014), forensic psychiatrists must translate these terms into plain language without sacrificing accuracy. For example, instead of simply stating that a defendant has “impaired insight,” the psychiatrist may explain that the individual does not recognize that they have a mental illness or that their actions were affected by their symptoms. This kind of accessible explanation allows legal professionals to follow the reasoning behind the psychiatric opinion.

Maintaining clarity also requires careful organization of testimony. Judges and juries often struggle to follow long, highly technical answers. Compelling testimony breaks information into smaller, understandable segments. According to Otto et al. (2014), the psychiatrist may begin by defining key terms, then explain how those definitions apply to the individual’s case, and finally connect those findings to the specific legal question at hand. Each part of the answer builds on the previous one, guiding the audience through the logic of the opinion step by step.

In addition to simplifying language, the psychiatrist must remain aware of nonverbal communication. According to Gottfried et al. (2014), jurors and judges not only listen to the expert’s words but also observe demeanor, body language, and emotional tone. Calm, measured speech conveys confidence and credibility. Nervousness, arrogance, or defensiveness, on the other hand, may distract from the content of the testimony and diminish its persuasive power. Maintaining steady eye contact, adopting a neutral posture, and speaking in a clear tone all contribute to a professional presentation that inspires trust.

One of the most critical aspects of courtroom communication is understanding the difference between legal and clinical standards. Legal decisions are based on statutes and case law that may not fully align with psychiatric models of understanding. For example, a defendant may have a severe mental illness yet still meet the legal standard for criminal responsibility. Gottfried et al. (2014) state that the psychiatrist must understand the legal criteria that govern the case and present psychiatric findings within that legal framework. It requires careful study of the relevant legal definitions before testifying. In court, the psychiatrist must be prepared to explain how the clinical data relates to each legal standard in simple, direct terms that judges and juries can apply in their deliberations.

Forensic psychiatrists must also be cautious not to speculate beyond the boundaries of their expertise or the available data. Judges and juries rely on expert testimony to clarify factual matters rather than to offer personal opinions or conjectures (Gottfried et al., 2014). When a question exceeds the psychiatrist's area of expertise or when data is insufficient to offer a conclusion, it is both ethical and professionally responsible to say so. Statements such as, "That is beyond the scope of my evaluation," or "I cannot offer an opinion based on the information available" demonstrate honesty and strengthen the expert's credibility.

During testimony, forensic psychiatrists may be tempted to act as educators, especially when explaining complex psychiatric phenomena. While providing necessary background information is appropriate, lengthy lectures or excessive technical detail can overwhelm legal audiences and risk losing their attention. Wathen (2005) states that the most effective testimony strikes a balance: it offers enough explanation for understanding without becoming a classroom lecture. Generally, short, focused answers that directly respond to the question are more effectively received by judges and juries.

Forensic psychiatrists must also be mindful of the emotional atmosphere of the courtroom. In many cases, legal proceedings involve serious allegations, high emotional tension, and public scrutiny. According to Wathen (2005), the expert must remain emotionally neutral, regardless of the nature of the offense or the conduct of the attorneys. Showing sympathy for one party or appearing dismissive toward another can raise concerns about bias. The expert's role is to serve the court, not either side of the case, and emotional neutrality helps reinforce this impartial stance.

Another essential element of effective communication is preparation. The psychiatrists should review the case file thoroughly before testifying, including their report, all collateral records, and any testing that was conducted. Snider et al. (2021) state that familiarity with the case allows the psychiatrist to answer questions confidently and without hesitation. Preparation also involves anticipating possible questions from both sides and considering how best to explain complex information in response. A well-prepared expert is far more likely to communicate effectively under the pressures of courtroom questioning.

In some cases, judges or juries may ask questions directly to clarify testimony. According to Snider et al. (2021), forensic psychiatrists should welcome these questions as an opportunity to ensure understanding. Answers should remain clear, focused, and respectful. If a question is unclear or misstates psychiatric facts, the psychiatrist may gently correct the misunderstanding while remaining respectful of the court's role.

Throughout all communication, honesty remains the guiding principle for the psychiatrist. Overstating certainty, minimizing limitations, or attempting to advocate for one side can severely damage credibility. Courts value experts who are careful, transparent, and willing to acknowledge both strengths and weaknesses in their opinions (Snider et al., 2021). Admitting when evidence is unclear or acknowledging alternative interpretations does not weaken testimony; instead, it shows professionalism and integrity.

Effective communication with judges and juries is as much a skill as clinical interviewing or report writing. It requires the ability to translate complex psychiatric information into accessible language, present findings clearly and confidently, and maintain emotional neutrality even under stressful circumstances. Forensic psychiatrists who develop strong courtroom communication skills make vital contributions to the justice system, ensuring that psychiatric evidence is understood and applied fairly in legal decision-making.

12.3 Managing Bias and Maintaining Professionalism

Forensic psychiatry operates at the intersection of medicine, law, and ethics. Forensic psychiatric evaluations are considered reliable when the psychiatrist is skilled, knowledgeable, impartial and professional. Bias, whether people are aware of it, is a major threat to the accuracy of forensic investigations. Rocchio (2020) points out that forensic psychiatrists should be aware of their biases, control and manage them to maintain objectivity, protect the law and follow ethical rules. It is important for forensic experts to be professional throughout the evaluation and testimony to ensure courts accept their opinions.

There are many ways that bias can affect forensic psychiatry. The first example is confirmation bias, where evaluators accept evidence that agrees with their first thoughts and ignore evidence which disagrees with them. For example, if a psychiatrist initially suspects malingering, they may overemphasize inconsistencies and underweight evidence of genuine mental illness. This selective attention can distort conclusions, even when the psychiatrist believes they are being objective and unbiased. Rocchio (2020) asserts that avoiding confirmation bias requires deliberate self-monitoring. Forensic psychiatrists must continuously test their working hypotheses against new information and actively seek data that could disprove their assumptions.

Another frequent source of bias is adversarial allegiance, where the evaluator unconsciously aligns with the party who retained them. Although forensic experts are intended to serve the court, they are often hired by either the prosecution, defense, plaintiff, or defense counsel in civil matters (Rocchio, 2020). This relationship may create pressure to produce opinions favorable to the hiring party. Even if not intentionally swayed, the psychiatrist may feel more sympathetic to the arguments or interpretations advanced by their referral source. Maintaining professional boundaries requires remembering that the evaluator's duty is not to the party who retained them but to the legal process itself.

Role confusion can also lead to bias. Some forensic psychiatrists, especially those who also maintain clinical practices, may slip into therapeutic habits during evaluations. According to Goldyne (2007), clinical psychiatrists naturally develop empathy, provide emotional support, and advocate for their patients' welfare. In forensic settings, however, this advocacy role is inappropriate and may cloud objectivity. Forensic psychiatrists must shift their role from caregiver to neutral evaluator. While it is essential to treat individuals respectfully and compassionately during evaluations, the primary goal is not treatment but an accurate and impartial assessment.

Bias may also stem from personal values or emotional reactions. For example, a psychiatrist's views about specific crimes, victims, or defendants may influence their attitudes toward the individual being evaluated. High-profile or emotionally charged cases, such as violent crimes, sexual offenses, or cases involving children, can provoke strong personal reactions. According to Goldyne (2007), forensic psychiatrists must recognize when such emotions are present and actively work to prevent them from affecting their analysis. Professional detachment is not the absence of human feeling but the discipline to keep personal feelings separate from professional judgment.

Beyond personal biases, forensic psychiatrists must also remain aware of systemic biases that can affect their work. According to Buongiorno et al. (2025), race, gender, socioeconomic status, cultural background, and language differences may influence how individuals present themselves, how their behavior is perceived, and how legal systems handle their cases. Forensic evaluators must consider cultural factors when interpreting behavior, symptom reporting, and risk assessments. Failure to do so can result in misdiagnosis, unfair conclusions, and harm to marginalized individuals. Training in cultural competence and continuous self-education are important safeguards against systemic bias.

Professionalism serves as both a foundation and a safeguard in managing bias. Professionalism is demonstrated through careful preparation, adherence to ethical guidelines, transparency in reasoning, and respectful communication. It also involves recognizing one's limits. Forensic psychiatrists should not offer opinions outside their area of expertise or beyond the information available (Buongiorno et al., 2025). When data is insufficient to support a firm conclusion, it is more professional to state that fact than to speculate about it.

A key professional practice is maintaining clarity in documentation. A well-written forensic report presents the conclusions and explains how those conclusions were reached. According to Rassin (2021), this transparency allows courts and opposing experts to review the psychiatrist's reasoning and test its validity. Clear documentation of all data reviewed, all methods used, and any limitations encountered help prevent accusations of bias or improper conduct.

Professionalism also means openness to scrutiny. Forensic psychiatrists should expect their work to be challenged by opposing counsel, reviewed by judges, and critiqued by other experts. According to Rassin (2021), psychiatrists must be willing to defend their conclusions with evidence, explain their reasoning under cross-examination, and acknowledge reasonable alternative interpretations when appropriate. Being open does not mean people are weak; instead, it shows they have strong ethical values.

It is also important to maintain professional boundaries with legal professionals. Forensic psychiatrists may be asked for advice by lawyers, but they should not be included in the team planning the legal strategy. The focus of talks with attorneys should be on the facts, the psychiatrist's opinion, and the applicable laws. Psychiatrists should not be influenced to say something positive in court, nor should they change their opinions to fit the case. They must provide an unbiased opinion to the court, regardless of which side hired them.

Professionalism also entails paying attention to how psychiatrists conduct themselves in the courtroom. Forensic psychiatrists should behave in a manner that demonstrates respect for the law and impartiality. Psychiatrists should dress professionally, use polite language, maintain a calm tone, and respond calmly, even if the other party attempts to provoke them. Rassin (2021) notes that a psychiatrist's behavior can impact how judges and juries perceive their testimony. Being calm and factual helps psychiatrists appear more credible and persuasive.

Forensic psychiatrists must always handle bias and maintain professionalism together. Bias may never be eliminated, but it can be recognized, managed, and minimized through ongoing self-awareness, adherence to ethical standards, and disciplined practice. Professionalism ensures that forensic psychiatrists contribute meaningful, fair, and trustworthy opinions that serve the interests of justice. These qualities not only strengthen the credibility of the psychiatrist but also uphold the integrity of the legal system as a whole.

12.4 Handling Challenging Legal Scenarios

Testifying as a forensic psychiatrist not only requires clinical expertise and effective communication but also the ability to manage unexpected and often difficult situations that can arise in court. According to Arboleda-Florez (2006), courtrooms are adversarial environments where attorneys may attempt to undermine expert testimony, other professionals may offer conflicting opinions, and complex legal dynamics may put pressure on even the most experienced expert. Being prepared for and managing challenging legal situations is crucial for maintaining a good reputation and trust in one's testimony.

Forensic psychiatrists often have to handle aggressive questioning from the other side during cross-examination. Attorneys might challenge the psychiatrists' qualifications, the way they work, or their conclusions by asking many questions in a short period, using sarcasm, or being confrontational. The purpose of these questions could be to make the expert feel uncomfortable or to make them contradict what they have said. Arboleda-Florez (2006) notes that in such situations, the psychiatrist should maintain a calm demeanor, pay close attention, and respond professionally. It is acceptable to pause before answering, ask for clarification if the question is unclear, and state "I don't know" when appropriate. Remaining emotionally neutral, even when under pressure, demonstrates control and enhances the psychiatrist's credibility in the eyes of the judge and jury.

A related challenge occurs when opposing counsel asks compound or misleading questions designed to trap the witness. According to Arboleda-Florez (2006), these questions may bundle multiple issues together, contain factual inaccuracies, or suggest conclusions not supported by evidence. The psychiatrist should focus on answering only what is being asked and avoid agreeing to inaccurate statements. If the question is confusing or mischaracterizes the facts, the expert may politely state, "That question contains several issues; let me address each separately," or "That does not accurately reflect my findings." Staying focused on the facts helps prevent being drawn into argumentative or speculative discussions.

Another frequent scenario is encountering conflicting expert testimony.In many cases, both sides in a legal dispute present expert witnesses who have reached different conclusions. Judges and juries may be presented with sharply contrasting opinions, leaving them to assess which expert is more credible and persuasive. When another expert disagrees with one's findings, the forensic psychiatrist needs to address these disagreements directly but respectfully. Eastman et al. (2013) state that the psychiatrist should clearly explain how their conclusions were reached, the data upon which they relied, and the reasoning that supports their opinion. Avoiding personal attacks on opposing experts preserves professionalism and demonstrates confidence in one's work.

At times, courts may appoint an independent expert when the two parties disagree on the evaluation. As Eastman et al. (2013) explained, in such cases, the psychiatrist is often asked to review the reports and give an unbiased opinion. Professionalism and objectivity are the most crucial qualities in this context. The psychiatrist needs to review all the information, accept arguments from both sides, and make a decision based on evidence rather than loyalty to any particular party.

When a psychiatrist testifies, it can be challenging if new information suddenly emerges. It may also include the addition of new records, evidence, or witness testimonies that were not accessible during the initial evaluation. According to Eastman et al. (2013), psychiatrists should carefully review the new information before providing further opinions. If the review period is short, the psychiatrists may request a break or inform the court that they need more time to review the new evidence before making a decision. Offering quick opinions without careful thought can make them less accurate and less believable.

Legal professionals may also attempt to challenge forensic psychiatrists' qualifications by questioning their expertise in a particular area, their training, or their experience with certain types of cases. In response, the psychiatrist should calmly outline their education, board certifications, relevant experience, and the number of similar evaluations they have performed. According to Raharjanti et al. (2021), providing a brief, factual summary of qualifications helps reaffirm the psychiatrist's authority without sounding defensive or boastful. It is also essential to recognize the limitations of one's expertise. For example, if a legal question involves highly specialized neuroimaging interpretation or complex financial matters outside the psychiatrist's training, it is appropriate to defer to experts in those fields.

Occasionally, attorneys may introduce hypothetical questions during cross-examination. These questions often propose alternate scenarios or assumptions designed to challenge the psychiatrist's conclusions. While answering hypothetical questions is allowed, the psychiatrist should carefully state whether the assumptions contained in the hypothetical are consistent with the facts of the case. If they are not, the psychiatrist should clarify that their original opinion was based on the actual evidence reviewed, and that a different set of facts may lead to a different conclusion. This distinction helps preserve the integrity of the psychiatrist's original opinion.

Handling ethically sensitive questions that arise during testimony is another challenging situation. Attorneys might ask about personal opinions, past statements in other cases, or even imagined political or moral beliefs to demonstrate that the expert is not neutral. Raharjanti et al. (2021) state that forensic psychiatrists should always keep their composure and steer the discussion back to the facts of the case. If someone asks about previous cases, the psychiatrist should provide concise, accurate answers that describe how each evaluation relied on its evidence. If patients attempt to challenge the psychiatrists' personal beliefs or political views, the psychiatrists should make it clear that their opinions are based solely on their professional training and evidence.

Sometimes, a forensic psychiatrist might notice that an attorney is behaving unethically, such as by coaching witnesses, concealing evidence, or attempting to intimidate experts outside the courtroom. When this happens, the psychiatrist should note the concerning behavior, consult with a lawyer, and, if required, inform the court or licensing authorities. Ethics should always take precedence over any specific case outcome.

Forensic psychiatrists should be prepared to handle cases that receive extensive media and public attention. Being in the media can bring extra pressure, change the way people perceive experts, and sometimes lead to criticism of their work. Raharjanti et al. (2021) state that in these situations, psychiatrists should maintain confidentiality, refrain from giving interviews to the media, and focus on their responsibilities to the court. When outside influences affect testimony or evaluation, the forensic process loses its objectivity and credibility.

Forensic psychiatrists deal with demanding legal matters. No matter how challenging the questions are and the presence of opposing experts or unexpected legal issues, the best option for forensic psychiatrists is to be well-prepared, stay calm and be objective. Forensic psychiatrists use facts, logic and ethical rules to assist courts in making the right decisions, no matter how tough the case is.

12.5 Summary and Takeaways

One of the most difficult tasks for forensic psychiatrists is to provide testimony in court. It involves knowing medicine, being prepared, clear in communication, being ethical and strong under stress. Psychiatrists should review the case documents, honestly assess their opinions and expect tough questions in depositions and cross examinations. The opposing side questions the psychiatrists who must explain psychiatric information in simple terms, and stay focused and calm.

Bias will always affect forensic work. Factors that make forensic psychiatrists to be biased must be known. These professionals should be impartial, follow the law, and explain their decisions clearly. Psychiatrists are expected to provide fair, supported and unbiased opinions to the court, even when they encounter difficult attorneys, opposing experts, or unexpected situations in court.

Psychiatrists bring valuable knowledge to the legal field when they prepare, communicate, and manage bias and professionalism well. They give clear, ethical and confident testimony to help courts make fair and well informed decisions about mental health and the law.

Chapter 13: Emerging Topics

New technologies and scientific findings are shaping forensic psychiatry and many other medical and legal fields. As new laws are developed, courts must decide how to include new types of evidence, assessment methods, and predictive tools in their decisions. Telepsychiatry, neuroimaging, genetics, and artificial intelligence are transforming forensic evaluations and the use of psychiatric evidence in courts. They offer new means to enhance access, accuracy, and efficiency. However, they can also raise ethical concerns, questions about their accuracy and questions about fairness, and privacy and the risk of misuse. These new developments should be known to forensic psychiatrists, their limitations understood and their impact on clinical practice, and legal testimony and the justice system considered. This chapter examines these new topics and how they are becoming increasingly important in the interface between psychiatry and law.

13.1 Telepsychiatry in Forensic Settings

Technological progress has enabled psychiatric care to be provided in more advanced ways than the traditional face to face sessions. In recent years, telepsychiatry which uses video conferencing and other remote methods for psychiatric care, has grown a lot. Derflinger et al. (2021) state that telepsychiatry is increasingly used in forensic psychiatry, especially when access to services is limited by distance, logistics or security.

Telepsychiatry is useful, but its use in forensic cases raises specific clinical, legal, and ethical concerns.

Forensic evaluations are easier to get with telepsychiatry. Onsite forensic psychiatric services are not available in many correctional facilities, detention centers, and rural areas. It is difficult, unsafe, and costly for the correctional system to move inmates or defendants to other facilities for assessment. Derflinger et al. (2021) state that telepsychiatry allows forensic psychiatrists to interview, assess, and consult from their offices. If mental health care is more accessible, it can prevent delays in assessments, prevent people from being held in jail without reason and support quicker decisions in court.

As Derflinger et al. (2021) explained, telepsychiatry allows forensic psychiatrists to reach people in underserved areas who might not otherwise have access to specialized care. In certain places, there may not be enough skilled forensic experts to handle evaluations promptly, particularly when the case involves unusual or complex legal issues. Telepsychiatry enables experts to consult from anywhere in the world, providing access to valuable guidance in complex cases.

Nevertheless, there are some obstacles to using telepsychiatry in forensic settings. A significant issue is the quality of the assessment design and its execution. Derflinger et al. (2021) state that in forensic evaluations, both spoken words and nonverbal signs, feelings, and small actions should be observed, as these may not always be clear on video. It is sometimes more challenging to spot psychomotor agitation, affective lability, or mild disorganization of thoughts. Sales et al. (2018) argue that if the video quality is poor, if there are delays in sound, or if the camera is not positioned correctly, it can be challenging for an evaluator to assess all the clinical features. For this reason, forensic psychiatrists who use telepsychiatry should take steps to ensure the person stays visible, try different camera angles, or ask more detailed questions during the interview.

Keeping information private and secure is also very important. Forensic evaluations require individuals to disclose private information, including their legal history and sometimes statements that could be used in court. Sales et al. (2018) stress that telepsychiatry platforms must be secure to ensure that patient privacy is protected and that health information is handled correctly. If a case is well-known or legally significant, unauthorized access, data breaches, or hacking can be particularly risky. To ensure security and adherence to the proper procedures, courts, attorneys, and forensic psychiatrists should all cooperate.

It is necessary to check if the evidence is admissible in a court of law. Courts sometimes wonder if a telepsychiatry evaluation is as reliable as one done face-to-face. It is possible to worry about how well the evaluator can assess the individual or whether remote interviews are a fair assessment method. Sales et al. (2018) state that, although telepsychiatric evaluations are now accepted in many places, the forensic psychiatrist must be prepared to clarify to the court how the review was conducted, why telepsychiatry was chosen, and how any issues were addressed. If necessary, additional documents or affidavits can be presented to support the use of telepsychiatric evidence in court.

Forensic telepsychiatry places particular importance on the concepts of voluntariness and informed consent. Gowda et al. (2020) state that individuals being evaluated should be advised that their interview is taking place remotely, that their information may be shared with legal officials, and that confidentiality is limited in court-ordered cases. Telepsychiatry platforms should have clear steps for obtaining and recording informed consent, which should cover the type of evaluation, any potential technical issues, and how patient data is secured.

Telepsychiatry has been adopted more widely in medicine, including forensic psychiatry, due to the COVID-19 pandemic. When it was not safe or possible to meet in person, courts allowed remote evaluations to help cases continue without delay. As a consequence, many places have continued to use telepsychiatry, mainly for initial meetings, regular assessments, and risk reviews, even after pandemic rules were relaxed.

However, not every forensic evaluation is appropriate for telepsychiatry. If the case involves important issues about malingering, competency, or complex psychotic symptoms, an in-person assessment may be helpful so the evaluator can observe the examinee's actions. In some critical cases, such as those involving capital punishment, civil commitment, or debated criminal responsibility, the standard remains to meet the person face-to-face (Sales et al., 2018). Forensic psychiatrists should look at every case on their own and team up with courts to decide when telepsychiatry is suitable and when a face-to-face evaluation is required.

Apart from individual assessments, telepsychiatry is now involved in other aspects of forensic work, such as providing expert opinions, participating in pretrial conferences, and testifying in court. In some instances, experts can provide testimony via secure video links when it is challenging for them to attend in person or when their input is required promptly during the trial (Sales et al., 2018). Even though remote testimony can save time, a forensic psychiatrist needs to remember that how they communicate is very important during these appearances. Being clear, having the right technology, and paying attention to body language is very important when talking to judges, attorneys, and juries over video.

Telepsychiatry can help increase access, lower costs, and improve the efficiency of forensic psychiatric evaluations. Nevertheless, when applied in forensic situations, it is important to pay close attention to clinical quality, security, legal rules, and ethics (Sales et al., 2018). With the development of telepsychiatry, forensic psychiatrists should be cautious to ensure that technology does not compromise the accuracy, fairness, or respect for individuals' rights within the legal system. Thoughtful and responsible use of telepsychiatry allows forensic psychiatry to serve more people without compromising its high standards.

13.2 Neuroimaging and Genetics in Legal Defenses

Discoveries in neuroscience have sparked increased interest in using neuroimaging and genetics in legal cases. Farahany (2016) notes that these new scientific tools are now being used in forensic psychiatry to support arguments in court, primarily for matters of criminal responsibility, sentencing, and risk assessment. While neuroimaging and genetics give psychiatrists many new opportunities, they also raise ethical, legal, and scientific issues. Even though these technologies can show how the brain works and the dangers of mental illness, their use in court is still not simple and is sometimes debated.

Neuroimaging utilizes advanced technology to visualize the structure and function of the brain. MRI (Magnetic Resonance Imaging), fMRI (functional MRI), PET (Positron Emission Tomography), and DTI (Diffusion Tensor Imaging) enable researchers and clinicians to study the brain's structure, blood flow, metabolism, and the connections between different brain regions. In some criminal cases, neuroimaging is used to claim that a person's actions are due to brain problems (Farahany, 2016). Defense teams can argue that brain areas responsible for impulse control, decision-making, and emotions were not functioning correctly in the person who committed the violent act.

When a legal case deals with traumatic brain injury (TBI), neuroimaging is commonly used. It may be used to demonstrate that if the frontal lobes are damaged in an MRI scan, the defendants struggle to control their impulses and comprehend the consequences of their actions.

Gkotsi et al. (2019) explain that individuals with issues in the amygdala or prefrontal cortex may struggle to control their emotions or aggression. In such cases, defense lawyers may claim that the brain dysfunction reduces the defendant's responsibility and supports asking for a reduced sentence.

Experts have tried to explain psychopathic behavior by using functional neuroimaging. It has been found that people with psychopathy have different brain activity in regions responsible for empathy, moral choices, and fear. Although these discoveries have garnered considerable attention, their application in specific criminal cases remains a topic of broad debate. Gkotsi et al. (2019) note that most experts believe neuroimaging research is not yet ready to predict a person's behavior or explain certain crimes. Since there are many ways biological, environmental, and personal factors can work together, the results from neuroimaging in forensic cases should be carefully considered.

Now, along with neuroimaging, genetic studies are being presented in court to help defendants. Genetic variations that make it more likely for someone to have psychiatric issues or act impulsively or aggressively have been identified. The monoamine oxidase A (MAOA) gene, also referred to as the "warrior gene," is the most frequently discussed example (McSwiggan et al., 2017). Individuals with low activity MAOA variants seem to be more prone to aggression if they have faced childhood maltreatment or trauma. Sometimes, defense lawyers use genetic evidence to argue that people's biological traits played a role in their actions and should be considered during sentencing or when determining their responsibility for the crime.

While these arguments are attractive, genetic evidence remains a subject of hotly contested debate in court. McSwiggan et al. (2017) argue that having a genetic variant does not mean that one will commit a crime; it is only one of many factors that may contribute to complex behavior. Genetic evidence can never prove cause or reduce responsibility due to the complex interplay of genetic, environmental, and personal factors. Usually, courts have been cautious with genetic defenses, recognizing that scientific evidence can be misused or overstated.

Neuroimaging and genetic research have brought up additional ethical issues. A primary concern is that determinism suggests that biology is the sole factor influencing behavior, thereby reducing personal responsibility. McSwiggan et al. (2017) state that neuroscience and genetics can help explain why some people are more likely to commit crimes, but they do not absolve individuals of personal responsibility. Courts must weigh scientific findings against established legal rules that require people to be responsible for their actions, regardless of their biology.

Fairness and equality are also important ethical issues in the law. Glannon (2014) points out that the use of advanced brain imaging and genetic testing can be influenced by a person's financial situation, which could give wealthier defendants an advantage in court. Similarly, using such evidence can unintentionally lead one to pay less attention to social, environmental, and psychological factors that are important for understanding behavior but lack clear biological signs.

A forensic psychiatrist must be familiar with both the scientific studies and the laws related to neuroimaging or genetic evidence. Glannon (2014) points out that the psychiatrist should judge if the evidence is based on science, important to the case, and handled with care. It involves checking the quality of the images, the techniques used to obtain them, and how any abnormalities found relate to the patient's condition (Glannon, 2014). For genetic evidence, the psychiatrist needs to assess the degree to which specific genetic variants are associated with behavior and the extent to which environmental factors influence behavior.

Forensic psychiatrists may be required to explain the limitations of neuroimaging and genetic evidence to courts, attorneys, and juries. It means pointing out that research is done on groups, not individuals, and that brain scans or genetic tests cannot explain each specific crime (Markowitsch&Staniloiu, 2011). The psychiatrist is responsible for providing the court with an objective, scientific explanation of how to assess the significance of such evidence.

In certain situations, neuroimaging and genetics are more useful in civil forensic cases, such as when determining personal injury or disability claims. If people claim cognitive impairment after a head injury, they may provide neuroimaging results to support their argument of brain damage (Markowitsch&Staniloiu, 2011). Even so, the forensic psychiatrist must verify whether the imaging results align with the reported symptoms and whether there are alternative explanations for the impairment.

Forensic psychiatry is seeing rapid progress in neuroimaging and genetics. Although these technologies may help explain brain function and behavior, they are not widely used in legal cases due to various scientific, ethical, and legal reasons. Forensic psychiatrists must assess whether the evidence is relevant, valid, and has any limitations, ensuring it is presented in a responsible manner (Markowitsch&Staniloiu, 2011). If used wisely, neuroimaging and genetics can help explain behavior, but they should always be considered together with the rest of psychiatric assessment and legal matters.

13.3 Technology in Forensic Psychiatry

Technology is changing nearly everything in modern society, and forensic psychiatry is no exception. De Looff et al. (2024) state that the use of advanced technology in forensics has significantly altered how psychiatric evaluations are conducted, how data are gathered and examined, and how experts present their opinions in court. While technology has been utilized in clinical psychiatry for some time, its application in forensic cases presents distinct opportunities and challenges that should be carefully considered. Using technology wisely in forensic psychiatry can enhance the accuracy, speed, and accessibility of evaluations; however, it can also introduce ethical, legal, and professional risks that forensic psychiatrists must manage.

The use of computers to keep records and analyze information has greatly changed forensic psychiatry. Forensic psychiatrists can handle information more smoothly because of the use of electronic records and secure databases. According to De Looff et al. (2024), these systems keep data safe and support easier comparison of data from different sources. An individual can use it to find matches in several documents such as common health problems, former diagnoses, or lawsuits with similar outcomes.

However, there are issues about how private, secure, and correct digital records can be. Forensic evaluations can collect very sensitive information and if the information is shared, it may harm the person being evaluated. According to Kirschstein et al. (2022), unauthorized use of electronic records can result in privacy issues and errors, or system problems may cause the information to be inaccurate. Kirschstein et al. (2022) recommend that forensic psychiatrists should team up with IT experts to secure digital records with strong security, encryption, and proper storage. Digital forensics should be done honestly, and all laws and ethical rules for data protection should be followed.

Forensic work now depends on technology to speed up psychological testing and assessment. Several paper tests have been converted into digital forms that can be handled by computers for administration, scoring, and interpretation. Kirschstein et al. (2022) state that using technology in assessment helps to avoid mistakes; results are always the same and are available immediately. Sometimes, digital testing platforms can spot people who are not honest about their symptoms.

However, there are several risks associated with using automated assessments. The results from the computer cannot replace the judgment of the forensic psychiatrist, and each person's evaluation should be interpreted individually. Kirschstein et al. (2022) note that automated scoring often overlooks cultural, developmental, and contextual factors that may impact test scores. Evaluators might also rely too heavily on computerized scores and fail to verify whether they align with what is observed or learned from other sources. The psychiatrist must consider the test results in light of the whole situation of the patient.

Forensic psychiatry now uses technology more for risk assessment and prediction, in addition to record-keeping and testing. Ogonah et al. (2023) note that the Violence Risk Appraisal Guide (VRAG) and the Historical Clinical Risk Management-20 (HCR-20) have been utilized for a considerable time to assess the likelihood of a person reoffending. Due to advances in data analytics, machine learning, and artificial intelligence, researchers can now utilize algorithms that analyze large datasets and identify patterns related to crime, treatment outcomes, and the risk of relapse.

These may assist in managing risks in legal and correctional settings. AI models could identify people who may commit another crime or have a mental health crisis, so they can get treatment sooner and more tailored. Risk assessment data is considered by courts in parole, civil commitment, and sentencing decisions.

However, numerous ethical and practical concerns are associated with the use of algorithmic risk assessment tools. Many of the models used for prediction are trained on data that may contain biases related to race, socioeconomic status, or other demographic factors. As a result, AI-based risk assessments may inadvertently perpetuate the existing imbalances in the legal system. Also, these models are often not very transparent about the process behind their predictions. Ogonah et al. (2023) advise that forensic psychiatrists should use algorithmic risk assessments with caution, recognizing their limitations and employing them in conjunction with, rather than in place of, detailed clinical assessments.

Technology has played a role in how experts share their opinions in court. Luxton et al. (2019) state that forensic psychiatrists can utilize video conferencing, digital tools for presentations, and electronic displays to present detailed information to judges and juries in an engaging manner. For instance, brain scans, charts showing the results of psychological tests or scores for assessing risks might be presented to explain what the experts think. Using visual aids can help jurors grasp psychiatric concepts that might be hard to understand.

Even though these tools make things clearer, they can also give the impression that things are certain. Luxton et al. (2019) argue that juries may pay more attention to eye-catching displays, especially when neuroimaging or statistics are involved in the case. Forensic psychiatrists should always clarify what the data means and what it cannot do so that judges and juries know these tools are only tools, not replacements for expert clinical opinion.

The use of technology has led to the creation of new digital evidence that is important in forensic psychiatric evaluations. Luxton et al. (2019) state that social media, text messages, emails, online searches, and electronic communications are now used in court to learn about a person's mood, intentions, or mental state. Sometimes, a forensic psychiatrist reviews these materials when assessing risks, evaluating criminal responsibility, or determining a person's civil capacity. It is important to be careful with digital evidence, since people's online actions might not show their real emotions and privacy should always be considered.

Technology helps forensic psychiatry by handling data, using standard tests, predicting risks, and assisting in court appearances. However, the advancements in medicine also lead to ethical, legal, and medical problems that require proper management. Luxton et al. (2019) state that forensic psychiatrists should watch out flaws and biases in technology. The use of technology must not interfere with the important roles of expertise, ethical behavior, and fairness in the legal field. If used in an ethical manner, technology assists forensic psychiatry by focusing on fairness, accuracy, and objectivity.

13.4 Artificial Intelligence and Risk Prediction in Forensic Psychiatry

Artificial intelligence (AI) has become a key subject in forensic psychiatry and often sparks conversations and disagreements. Parmigiani et al. (2024) suggest that there are rising issues in law and mental health because of machine learning and predictive analytics. They are programmed to spot risks, examine files closely, and deal with a massive amount of data in less time than what an individual can do. Besides, such actions bring up ethical, legal, and scientific issues that are against the core values of forensic psychiatry.

By relying on data and analyzing it, AI learns about new things, notices patterns, makes sense of what it knows, and provides suggestions. Parmigiani et al. (2024) state that these abilities are essential in forensic psychiatry since they help predict whether a person will commit violence, other crimes, or react to treatment appropriately. Forensic psychiatry includes assessing risk and AI can analyze greater amounts of data than a person.

When using clinical knowledge or statistical data of a few research factors, the HCR-20 and Static-99 are used. Alternatively, AI algorithms might consider psychiatric history, factors in a person's social life, history of crimes, biological analysis, and the use of internet. Parmigiani et al. (2024) explain that machine learning algorithms can link all pieces of data and discover relationships that standard clinical practice might not notice. As a result, it might reveal people at risk of causing another crime, getting therapy, self-harming, or harming others.

Some legal settings already have AI-based risk prediction systems in practice. Algorithmic tools have been employed in some jurisdictions to aid in bail decisions, parole eligibility assessments, or sentencing recommendations. Predictive models have been explored in forensic psychiatric hospitals to guide discharge planning, identify patients at risk of decompensation, and inform the development of individualized treatment plans (Parmigiani et al., 2024). Sometimes, AI helps identify individuals who may require additional attention or assists doctors in making decisions about high-risk cases.

A significant issue is that predictive algorithms can be biased. As Van Le et al. (2018) explained, the data used to train AI systems determines the objectivity of the resulting systems. If historical data in AI models contain existing disparities, the models may end up reproducing or exacerbating these disparities. For example, suppose a machine learning system is trained on criminal justice data that contains patterns of over-policing or unequal sentencing. In that case, it will generate risk scores that disproportionately label some groups as high-risk, regardless of their actual characteristics.

It raises significant ethical issues of justice and equality in the law. Forensic psychiatrists should exercise caution in not relying too heavily on AI-based risk scores, as these could replace personal evaluations or support unjust actions. Van Le et al. (2018) argue that since AI systems may be biased, they should be made transparent. Courts, attorneys, and defendants should know how risk scores are determined and what goes into them. Unfortunately, a lot of AI models do not explain the process they use to get results. If data is not openly shared, science and the justice system lose their credibility.

It is risky that AI could be overused in forensic psychiatry to predict results. Tay et al. (2024) point out that algorithms can spot patterns, but they do not grasp fully the details of human actions, decisions, or the setting of crimes. Predictive models are based on probability, not on absolute certainty. A person who is flagged as high risk might never commit another crime, but someone seen as low risk can still do harm. If people depend too much on AI predictions, they may think the statistics are more accurate than they really are and overlook the details of each case.

AI models often have trouble dealing with the changing risk factors that are important in psychiatric assessments. According to Tay et al. (2024), forensic psychiatrists regularly assess insight, motivation, a person's level of engagement in treatment, family support, and recent stressors, as these factors can all change and impact risk. Although some advanced AI models attempt to incorporate changing aspects, they are still unable to replicate the detailed clinical judgment employed by skilled forensic psychiatrists.

There are legal issues that coming up in the use of AI in forensics. It is challenging for courts to decide if algorithmic risk scores can be used, especially when the models are not made public or have not been looked at by experts. Defense lawyers might argue that AI-generated evidence is not fair or reliable, while prosecutors may try to rely on it to seek harsher sentences or more supervision. Tay et al. (2024) state that forensic psychiatrists should be prepared to explain the advantages and disadvantages of these models, how they used the data, and why they made the decisions without relying on AI.

Privacy is also a major issue. Usually, AI models use information like medical and criminal records, employment data, content from social media, and digital records when they are trained. Parmigiani et al. (2024) mention that when sensitive data is collected, stored, and analyzed, there are major concerns about obtaining consent, ensuring confidentiality and the possibility of misuse. Safeguards are required to ensure people's rights are respected and data is not abused.

Various groups of experts are now establishing guidelines for the use of AI in forensics. Parmigiani et al. (2024) state that AI tools should be used in conjunction with clinical assessments, should be easy to understand, and that bias should be monitored. It is up to the forensic psychiatrist to provide conclusions to the court, and they cannot depend on technology to make those decisions.

There are some challenges, but AI is expected to play a significant role in forensic psychiatry. Parmigiani et al. (2024) believe that if AI is used carefully, with the assistance of clinicians, lawyers, ethicists, and data scientists, it can enhance the accuracy and fairness of forensic evaluations. Machine learning may identify risks that are not immediately apparent, suggest personalized treatments, or detect early signs of psychiatric issues. However, these advantages will only be realized if forensic psychiatrists remain responsible and ethical with AI, so it does not negatively affect the justice system.

13.5 Summary and Takeaways

Forensic psychiatry is undergoing rapid changes due to the impact of technology and new scientific findings on clinical work, assessments, and court testimony. With telepsychiatry, experts can now provide forensic evaluations to courts and correctional facilities in various locations, but it raises concerns about confidentiality, the ability of the expert to observe, and informed consent. Though neuroimaging and genetics reveal information about the brain and genetics, they are not yet able to explain personal responsibility or accurately predict a person's behavior. Forensic psychiatrists ought to be careful and present the evidence from mental health research correctly.

With technology, processes such as storing records on computers, automated assessments, and analyzing data have improved the consistency and labor cost-effectiveness of forensic work. Psychiatrists have to keep a close eye on them to avoid any misuse, too much use, or issues of ethics. Although artificial intelligence aids in risk prediction and working with large datasets, it may introduce biases, reduce transparency, and hinder the use of personal evaluations. Forensic psychiatrists must apply their professional judgment, ethics, and fairness whenever employing new technologies. Applying recent approaches while sticking to their key values, forensic psychiatrists can address these changes and keep assisting the legal system.

Chapter 14: Case Studies and Practical Scenarios

Forensic psychiatry is often concerned with cases that require expertise in both psychiatric and legal fields. Such decisions involve determining who is responsible for a crime, assessing the risk a person poses, whether someone is capable of making decisions, or who will care for a child. While it is essential to understand the diagnostic criteria, laws, and theories, the real challenge in forensic psychiatry lies in applying this knowledge to real people in legal contexts. Every case presents its unique facts, psychological issues, and legal matters, which require the forensic psychiatrist to be careful, objective, and adhere to ethical and legal standards.

Forensic psychiatry is used in practice by considering both a person's mental health and how the findings relate to the law. It involves collecting a large amount of information, studying detailed histories, and employing a careful approach to form informed opinions that are crucial in law. It is also essential for forensic psychiatrists to clearly and convincingly explain their findings to courts, attorneys, and other legal professionals so that psychiatric input contributes to fair and just legal decisions.

This chapter presents several case studies that demonstrate how the main principles from this book are applied in actual forensic work. They illustrate the various situations that psychiatrists working in criminal courts, civil litigation, family law, and correctional settings often encounter. Every case points out major psychiatric, legal, and ethical issues, stressing the need for individual assessments, fair decision-making, and professional impartiality in forensic psychiatry.

14.1 Case 1: Fitness to Stand Trial – Intellectual Disability

A 22-year-old woman named Ms. Emily Davis was arrested when she was found in a department store after the store had closed. Ms. Davis was discovered by security staff in the stockroom, looking confused and unable to explain how she had entered the store. Police said she was polite and cooperative, but her answers regarding her intentions were not always consistent. She was accused of burglary, and her lawyer immediately argued that she might not understand the legal process.

Ms. Davis was diagnosed with developmental disability when she was a child. Her school records showed that she had always been in special education, where she received personalized help with learning and daily living. Her previous psychological tests showed that her full-scale IQ was 65, which is considered mild intellectual disability. Family members explained that Emily needed constant help each day for things like handling money, getting around, and knowing how to behave in social situations.

Ms. Davis had trouble understanding the questions about her legal situation during the forensic evaluation. She could not explain the role of the judge or attorneys in her case and found it very hard to understand what she was being charged with. When someone asked her what burglary meant, she just replied, "It's not good, I believe." She did not know what plea bargaining was and could not list the possible outcomes of being convicted, always saying she was sure she would return home soon.

She also experienced difficulties with abstract thinking, paying attention, and recalling information for a short period. She would often say "yes" or "I don't know" if she was not sure, and she would try to guess instead of admitting she did not understand.

Discussion

The main issue in Ms. Davis' case was whether she was capable of understanding and joining in the trial. The law generally requires the defendants to be competent by showing that they can do the following:

- Understand the nature and purpose of the legal proceedings.
- Recognize the roles of legal personnel.
- Be able to assist counsel in preparing a defense.
- Appreciate the potential consequences of legal outcomes.

Although Ms. Davis was helpful, her answers showed that she did not understand how the legal system works. She was unable to understand the difference between guilt and innocence, the roles of those involved in court, or what happens during sentencing. Due to her cognitive issues, she was unable to participate in discussions with her attorney or make informed decisions regarding legal matters.

Notably, forensic evaluators must distinguish between mere unfamiliarity and genuine incompetence. Ms. Davis' deficits went beyond simple unfamiliarity; her intellectual disability limited her ability to acquire and retain new legal information, even after repeated explanations. Structured interviews and competency screening instruments confirmed that she failed to meet minimal competency standards.

The evaluation also examined whether competency restoration efforts would be successful. In some cases, defendants with intellectual disabilities can improve their legal understanding with targeted educational interventions. However, Ms. Davis' intellectual profile suggested that restoration would likely be unsuccessful due to her globally impaired reasoning, poor memory retention, and limited adaptive functioning.

Ethically, the forensic psychiatrist must ensure that evaluations of competency are based on current functioning rather than relying solely on diagnostic labels. Intellectual disability alone does not automatically render a defendant incompetent; however, in Ms. Davis' case, her deficits impaired her ability to participate in the legal process.

Ms. Davis lacked the functional understanding and reasoning abilities required to stand trial. The psychiatrist's report provided the court with clear documentation of her intellectual disability, cognitive limitations, and poor legal comprehension. The findings supported a recommendation that she be found incompetent to proceed, with additional consideration for long-term guardianship and supervision rather than ongoing criminal prosecution.

14.2 Case 2: Criminal Responsibility – Schizophrenia and the Insanity Defense

Mr. David Matthews, aged 29, was arrested for second-degree murder after he stabbed and killed a stranger, Mr. Robert Jenkins, in a public park. The event took place in broad daylight and was seen by many people nearby. After his arrest, Mr. Matthews said to the officers that Mr. Jenkins belonged to a secret group that had put devices in his body to control his mind. He claimed that he was told by voices to kill the enemy to stop global harm.

Mr. Matthews was diagnosed with schizophrenia about seven years before the incident. His medical documents revealed that he was hospitalized several times for psychotic episodes, with symptoms such as persecutory delusions, hearing voices, and disordered speech. Mr. Matthews had a long record of not following the antipsychotic medications he was given. According to his family, he had become more isolated and more suspicious and declined to see a psychiatrist in the months before the offense.

The court ordered a forensic psychiatric evaluation to assess his criminal responsibility. During the review, Mr. Matthews appeared disheveled and disorganized. He demonstrated thought blocking, loose associations, and paranoia. He continued to express firm beliefs that various government agencies were targeting him and that Mr. Jenkins was an "agent" sent to harm him. Mr. Matthews displayed poor insight into his condition and lacked an understanding of the nature of the legal charges against him.

Discussion

The legal question in Mr. Matthews' case centered on his criminal responsibility at the time of the offense. Under the applicable legal standard, similar to the M'Naghten rule, the evaluation focused on whether Mr. Matthews, due to his mental illness, lacked the capacity to appreciate the nature and wrongfulness of his conduct during the homicide.

Mr. Matthews' extensive psychotic symptoms, including auditory command hallucinations and fixed persecutory delusions, suggested that his reality testing was profoundly impaired at the time of the offense. He did not perceive the victim as an innocent stranger but as part of a threatening conspiracy targeting him. His actions were driven by an effort to defend himself against imagined harm rather than malicious intent.

Collateral information provided strong support for the forensic opinion. Police reports, witness statements, psychiatric records, and family interviews confirmed his longstanding schizophrenia, patterns of decompensation, and non-adherence to treatment. It confirmed that his psychotic disorder was ongoing and severe.

It was essential to carefully examine for malingering since this is a common concern in forensic evaluations involving psychosis and criminal responsibility. Mr. Matthews' delusions were stable, well-recorded for years, and included formal thought disorder and cognitive disorganization, which are hard to fake.

In addition to considering criminal responsibility, the evaluation looked at Mr. Matthews' ability to take part in the trial. Because he did not understand his role in court, the charges, or how to defend himself, it was decided he should not continue. Even though psychiatric treatment could help restore competency, his severe psychosis at the time of the assessment made him temporarily unable to understand the proceedings.

The case of Mr. Matthews shows that chronic schizophrenia can lead to impaired criminal responsibility because of active psychosis. The forensic psychiatrist was responsible for bringing together the facts from the case, Mr. Matthews's history, and legal rules to help the court decide if he was legally insane. It demonstrates the need for a thorough review that combines medical and legal aspects in challenging criminal cases.

14.3 Case 3: Child Custody Evaluation – Parental Mental Illness

Mr. Thomas Reynolds and Mrs. Laura Reynolds divorced after twelve years of marriage and entered a legal dispute over the custody of their two children, 8-year-old Olivia and 11-year-old Ethan. Mr. Reynolds sought full custody, citing concerns over Mrs. Reynolds' history of bipolar I disorder. He argued that her mental illness presented ongoing risks to the children's safety and emotional well-being. In contrast, Mrs. Reynolds petitioned for joint custody, emphasizing her treatment compliance and a long period of stability.

Mrs. Reynolds was diagnosed with bipolar I disorder approximately eight years earlier. Her psychiatric history included three hospitalizations for manic episodes during the first few years following diagnosis. Medical records documented manic symptoms, including pressured speech, impulsivity, grandiosity, financial overspending, and sleep deprivation during those episodes. Over the past four years, however, Mrs. Reynolds had been stable on mood-stabilizing medication, consistently attended outpatient therapy, and had no psychiatric hospitalizations.

The forensic evaluation involved separate interviews with both parents, observations of parent-child interactions, individual interviews with Olivia and Ethan, review of medical and psychiatric records, and interviews with collateral sources such as teachers, pediatricians, and extended family members.

During their interviews, both children described strong emotional bonds with both parents. Olivia stated that her mother helped her with homework, cooked meals, and attended school events. Ethan reported that his mother took him to sports practices and helped with his music lessons. Both children recalled periods in the past when their mother had been "very sick" and in the hospital, but they described the current home environment as safe, loving, and stable. Neither child reported recent incidents of mood instability or concerning parental behavior.

Mr. Reynolds said that Mrs. Reynolds had been stable for some time, but he was concerned that the stress of co-parenting and the divorce could cause her to have another manic episode. He argued that giving sole custody to one parent would be more stable for the children.

Mrs. Reynolds admitted to having been hospitalized before and clearly understood her condition. She talked about spotting early signs of mood changes and introduced her strong support team, which included her psychiatrist, therapist, family, and friends. She assured the court that she would continue to parent, follow the treatment plan, and ensure the children's safety.

Discussion

During custody evaluations, the focus should be on the parent's current mental state, not only on their past diagnoses. Just having bipolar disorder does not prevent a parent from being considered for shared custody. Instead, evaluators should pay attention to the following:

- Stability of psychiatric condition.
- Insight into illness.
- Compliance with treatment.
- Parenting abilities.
- Presence of supportive structures.
- Potential impact of relapse on child well-being.

Mrs. Reynolds demonstrated a stable, insightful, and compliant attitude toward treatment for many years. There was no sign that the parents had recently struggled or were unable to care for their children. The kids described their environment as safe and caring. Their teachers and pediatricians reported that both Olivia and Ethan were doing well in school and emotionally, without any concerns about neglect or misbehavior.

Bipolar disorder can sometimes return if the person experiences a lot of stress. Still, if there is no current impairment, the risk alone does not deprive parents of their legal rights or their best interests. Her adherence to psychiatric care, having support around her, and her relapse prevention strategies helped a lot in reducing this risk.

The forensic psychiatrist was required to give an unbiased, well-supported assessment to help the court decide what custody plan was best for the children. The evaluation showed that Mrs. Reynolds could safely share custody with her ex-husband. The psychiatrist made it clear that Mrs. Reynolds' stable condition, good compliance, and good insight were much more critical than any speculative concerns about relapse.

Although Mr. Reynolds had valid concerns, the overall evidence indicated that Mrs. Reynolds remained a suitable parent. The recommendation was for joint custody, and the court could review the arrangement if the mother's mental health worsened. It shows that, when appropriately managed, parental mental illness should not always result in losing parental rights, but each situation should be carefully examined.

14.4 Case 4: Violence Risk Assessment – Sexual Offender

Five years ago, Mr. Michael Turner was found guilty of sexually assaulting Ms. Angela Peterson, who he attacked while she was jogging in a public park. Mr. Turner grabbed Ms. Peterson, dragged her into the woods, and sexually assaulted her while threatening her with harm. He was arrested shortly afterward and admitted everything during questioning. The judge ordered him to serve a prison sentence.

Mr. Turner had no prior history of sexual offenses. However, his criminal record included two prior non-violent charges for shoplifting and public intoxication. He reported a history of substance abuse, primarily alcohol, which was active during the time of the sexual assault. He attributed his offending behavior, in part, to his impaired judgment during intoxication.

As Mr. Turner approached parole eligibility, the parole board requested a comprehensive risk assessment to determine his suitability for conditional release. A forensic psychiatrist was assigned to conduct the evaluation, focusing on his likelihood of sexual reoffending and general violence risk.

During incarceration, Mr. Turner had fully completed a sex offender treatment program, regularly attended substance abuse counseling, and consistently engaged with prison psychiatrists. Institutional records reflected excellent behavior, no disciplinary infractions, and active participation in rehabilitation efforts. He remained abstinent from substances throughout his incarceration.

The forensic evaluation included the administration of several standardized risk assessment tools. The Static-99R, an actuarial tool for predicting sexual offense recidivism in adult males, was used. Mr. Turner scored in the moderate risk category based on factors such as his victim being a stranger, his age, and lack of stable intimate relationships before incarceration. The Stable-2007 assessment was used to assess factors that can change over time. Mr. Turner's Stable-2007 scores showed that he could manage his emotions, interact socially, solve problems, and accept responsibility, which is positive progress in therapy.

The team interviewed his therapists, substance abuse counselors, family members, and the people who would supervise him on parole. His doctors and therapists said he was very active in treatment, wanted to improve, and was always remorseful and showed responsibility for what he did. After his release, his family offered him a house, assisted him in chores and his older brother, Mr. Daniel Turner, regularly supervised him.

Mr. Turner knew how his offenses happened, openly talked about his past distorted thinking, and created a detailed plan to avoid relapsing. He identified social isolation, substance use, and unsupervised unstructured time as high-risk factors and outlined strategies to manage these triggers through continued therapy, family involvement, structured employment, and ongoing substance abuse monitoring.

Discussion

The primary purpose of the violence risk assessment was not to predict Mr. Turner's exact future behavior but rather to assist the parole board in estimating the likelihood of reoffending and determining appropriate supervision conditions upon release. Risk assessment combines both static factors (unchangeable historical variables) and dynamic factors (changeable present or future variables).

Mr. Turner's Static-99R score placed him at a moderate risk level based on population data. However, risk assessment cannot rely solely on actuarial scores. His Stable-2007 evaluation provided valuable information regarding his current functioning, personal insight, and ability to apply treatment gains. His meaningful engagement in therapy, willingness to accept responsibility, and consistent abstinence all supported significant progress.

Evaluating the company required reviewing additional information. Treatment providers, family members, and staff at the prison all reported that Mr. Turner wanted to change for the better. Having a strong support network after release supervised him, held him accountable, and helped him adjust to life outside prison.

Even so, the fact that his first victim was a stranger in a public area was a significant risk factor for the future. Assaults against strangers are more likely to be followed by another offense than assaults against people known to the offender. Moving from a prison to a community setting can be difficult for some people if they do not have enough support.

The forensic psychiatrist pointed out that there is no way to be certain with any assessment tool. The recommendation to the parole board was based on weighing Mr. Turner's progress with the risks from his past. It was found that safe parole release depends on structured supervision, continued therapy, monitoring substance abuse, and having external support.

Specific recommended conditions included the following:

- Ongoing outpatient sex offender therapy.
- Regular substance abuse testing.
- Structured employment and community activities.

- Supervised housing with family oversight.
- Restricted access to unsupervised public recreational areas.
- Immediate reporting of any relapse triggers or concerning behaviors.

Mr. Turner's situation demonstrates how complicated it can be to assess forensic risk in sexual offending. Even though static factors help predict the risk, dynamic changes, sticking to treatment, having support and detailed plans for relapse help ensure a safe return to the community. The forensic psychiatrist's job is to give a fair and unbiased opinion that helps make public safety decisions and supports the individual's rehabilitation.

14.5 Case 5: Testamentary Capacity – Early Dementia

Mrs. Margaret Collins, who is 76 and retired, made a new will that excluded her two eldest children, James and Susan, and gave all her assets to her youngest son, Daniel. After their mother's death, James and Susan argued that she was not mentally capable of making a will because of her dementia. The court appointed a forensic psychiatrist to look back at Mrs. Collins' mental state when she made the will.

Mrs. Collins was diagnosed with early-stage Alzheimer's disease about a year before the will was written. Her primary care physician and neurologist noted that her memory was declining slowly, she had trouble finding words at times, and she had some difficulty with complex tasks such as handling money. She was still able to live by herself, hold her medications, and go to her medical appointments without help. James and

Susan said they had significant memory problems, but Daniel and the healthcare team said he was mostly stable.

The forensic psychiatrist looked at a lot of information, including previous neuropsychological tests, medical and psychiatric records, legal documents, and interviews with Mrs. Collins' family, her attorney, and healthcare workers. Six months before the will was signed, a neuropsychological evaluation showed that the person had some memory problems but was still able to reason, understand, and manage tasks.

It was found through collateral interviews that Mrs. Collins and her two eldest children have conflicted for a long time, mainly because of disagreements over money and caregiving after her husband passed away. On the other hand, Daniel Collins helped his mother daily, handled household tasks, and provided her with emotional support as she was ill. Several people close to Mrs. Collins said that she clarified for years that she wanted to leave Daniel her entire estate for his care and loyalty.

Mrs. Collins' attorney, Mr. William Harper, conducted a detailed assessment of her understanding and intentions on the day of the will signing. His contemporaneous notes recorded that Mrs. Collins accurately identified her children, described her financial assets, clearly articulated the reasons for her decisions, and expressed confidence in her choices. Mr. Harper reported no indications of confusion, coercion, or impaired comprehension during their meeting.

Discussion

The central legal question was whether Mrs. Collins possessed testamentary capacity when she executed her will. The legal standard for testamentary capacity generally requires that individuals do the following:

- Understand that they are making a will.
- Know the nature and extent of their property.
- Recognize the natural beneficiaries of their estate.
- Understand how their property will be distributed.
- Make decisions free from undue influence or delusions affecting the distribution.

Importantly, a diagnosis of Alzheimer's disease does not automatically invalidate testamentary capacity. Instead, capacity is evaluated based on the individual's ability to function at the specific time of the will's execution. Many individuals in the early stages of dementia retain sufficient understanding to make complex decisions when appropriately supported.

In this case, the totality of evidence strongly indicated that Mrs. Collins possessed the necessary cognitive capacity. Despite mild memory impairment, she demonstrated intact reasoning, consistent expression of her wishes, and complete knowledge of her financial circumstances. Her motivations for disinheriting James and Susan were longstanding and well-documented, not impulsive or based on delusional thinking. The attorney's records provided particularly persuasive contemporaneous evidence of her clarity and decisional capacity on the day of signing.

The claims raised by James and Susan primarily emphasized the existence of dementia itself rather than offering evidence that her condition rendered her incapable of making reasoned decisions. The forensic evaluation emphasized that cognitive impairment must be assessed along a spectrum, recognizing that individuals may maintain capacity even in the presence of early memory deficits if other cognitive domains remain intact.

Besides checking the person's mental state, the forensic psychiatrist also examined if any outside pressure influenced the will. Several independent sources showed that Mrs. Collins acted willingly, grateful for Daniel Collins' care, and not because she was forced or tricked.

The forensic psychiatrist determined that Mrs. Collins possessed the mental capacity to make a will when she did so. She made her decisions based on her long-held intentions, not because of any mental impairment or outside pressure.

14.6 Summary and Takeaways

These case studies highlight the many challenging and sensitive cases that forensic psychiatrists encounter. Whenever a situation arises, it needs several clinical skills, understanding the law, ethical duties, and clear thinking. In every situation, such as assessing responsibility, competency, parenting, and violence risk or capacity, a forensic psychiatrist must gather complete information, consider different opinions, and clearly report the findings to legal professionals. Forensic psychiatry must follow the law, which calls for accuracy and impartiality. Psychiatric diagnoses should be offered as opinions to help the courts decide on a case. They explain why it is necessary to consider the special circumstances, background, and legal matters of every individual. With the progress of science and the law, studying real cases is one of the best ways forensic psychiatrists can be ready for real-world situations. Looking at various cases allows forensic psychiatrists to offer fair, detailed, and reliable evaluations that help their patients and the justice system.

References

Achilli, F., Leo, S., Benatti, B., Frediani, A., Cocchi, M., Molteni, L., Piccoli, E., Lana, M., Lucchini, E., Gobbo, D., &Dell'Osso, B. M. (2024). Criminal behaviors and substance use disorder in psychiatric patients. *CNS Spectrums*, 1–25. doi: 10.1017/s1092852924000373

Al Jowf, G. I., Ahmed, Z. T., Reijnders, R. A., de Nijs, L., &Eijssen, L. M. T. (2023). To predict, prevent, and manage post-traumatic stress disorder (PTSD): A review of pathophysiology, treatment, and biomarkers. *International Journal of Molecular Sciences*, *24*(6), 1–31. doi: 10.3390/ijms24065238

Alkema, A., Marchi, M., Van Der Zaag, J. A., Van Der Sluis, D., Warrier, V., Ophoff, R. A., ... & Genetic Risk and Outcome of Psychosis (GROUP) Investigators (2024). Childhood abuse v. neglect and risk for major psychiatric disorders. *Psychological Medicine*, *54*(8), 1–12. doi: 10.1017/S0033291723003471.

Amer A. B. (2013). Informed consent in adult psychiatry. *Oman Medical Journal*, 28(4), 228–231. doi: 10.5001/omj.2013.67

American Academy of Psychiatry and the Law (AAPL).(2015). *Practice guidelines for forensic psychiatric evaluation.* https://aapl.org/docs/pdf/Forensic_Assessment.pdf

Aravind, H., Taylor, M., & Gill, N. (2024). Evaluation of testamentary capacity: A systematic review. International *Journal of Law and Psychiatry*, 93.doi: 10.1016/j.ijlp.2024.101969

Arboleda-Florez, J. (2006). Forensic psychiatry: contemporary scope, challenges and controversies. *World Psychiatry*, 5(2), 87–91. https://pmc.ncbi.nlm.nih.gov/articles/PMC1525122/

Baillargeon, J., Binswanger, I. A., Penn, J. V., Williams, B. A., & Murray, O. J. (2009). Psychiatric disorders and repeat incarcerations: The revolving prison door. *American Journal of Psychiatry, 166*(1), 103–109. doi: 10.1176/appi.ajp.2008.08030416

Barbosa-Torres, C., Bueso-Izquierdo, N., &Cubo-Delgado, S. (2023). Analysis of malingered psychological symptoms in a clinical sample for early detection in initial interviews.*European Archives of Psychiatry and Clinical Neuroscience*, *273*(2), 427–438. doi: 10.1007/s00406-022-01422-8

Barroso, R., Pham, T., Greco, A. M., &Thibaut, F. (2019).Challenges in the treatment of sex offenders.*Long-Term Forensic Psychiatric Care*, 169–180. doi: 10.1007/978-3-030-12594-3_12

Bellman, V., Chinthalapally, A., Johnston, E., Russell, N., Bruce, J., &Saleem, S. (2022). Malingering of psychotic symptoms in psychiatric settings: Theoretical aspects and clinical considerations.*Psychiatry Journal*, *2022*, 1–9. doi: 10.1155/2022/3884317

Bernath, B. (2021). The new principles on effective interviewing for investigations and information gathering– an overview.*Torture Journal*, *31*(3), 121–126. doi: 10.7146/torture.v32i3.129960

Bickle, A., Cameron, C., Hassan, T., Safdar, H., &Khalifa, N. (2021).International overview of phallometric testing for sexual offending behaviour and sexual risk.*Bjpsych International*, 18(4). https://www.cambridge.org/core/journals/bjpsych-international/article/international-overview-of-phallometric-testing-for-sexual-offending-behaviour-and-sexual-risk/205871CC4967C793F7238E45882622B0

Boonmann, C., Schmeck, K., & Witt, A. (2024).Forensic child & adolescent psychiatry and psychology in Europe.*Child and Adolescent Psychiatry and Mental Health*, 18(1).doi: 10.1186/s13034-024-00756-6

Brady, C., Burgess, R. A., &Osrin, D. (2022). Understanding diversion programmes as an intervention for women with mental health issues: A realist review. *SSM - Mental Health, 2*.doi: 10.1016/j.ssmmh.2022.100066

Brannick, M. E. (2015). *Guidelines for forensic report writing: Helping trainees understand common pitfalls to improve reports*. https://digitalcommons.du.edu/cgi/viewcontent.cgi?article=1062&context=capstone_masters

Buchanan A. (2004). Mental capacity, legal competence and consent to treatment. *Journal of the Royal Society of Medicine*, 97(9), 415–420. doi: 10.1177/014107680409700902

Bullough, C., Leach, C., & Harden, S. (2021). Assessing fitness for trial in a Children's Court.*Psychiatry, Psychology and Law*, 29(3).doi: 10.1080/13218719.2021.1910587

Buongiorno, L., Mele, F., Petroni, G., Margari, A., Carabellese, F., Catanesi, R., &Mandarelli, G. (2025). Cognitive biases in forensic psychiatry: A scoping review. *International Journal of Law and Psychiatry, 101*.doi: 10.1016/j.ijlp.2025.102083

Burgess, B. (2024, August 20). *An evaluation of fitness to stand trial assessment practices across Canada*. University of Manitoba.

https://mspace.lib.umanitoba.ca/items/aaa3ca98-4b10-45b1-8111-ff33c8398a81

Candilis, P. J., & Martinez, R. (2021). The revolution in forensic ethics: Narrative, compassion, and a robust professionalism. *Psychiatric Clinic of North America*, 44(4), 571-578. https://www.researchgate.net/profile/Philip-Candilis/publication/26257604_The_Revolution_in_Forensic_Ethics_Narrative_Compassion_and_a_Robust_Professionalism/links/634dac376e0d367d91a5e6a8/The-Revolution-in-Forensic-Ethics-Narrative-Compassion-and-a-Robust-Professionalism.pdf

Cerny-Suelzer, C. A., Michaelsen, K., Wasser, T., Kushner, D., & Friedman, S. H. (2024).Forensic psychiatry as a key part of residency training in social justice and mental health inequities.*AcademicPsychiatry*.doi: 10.1007/s40596-024-01989-5

Chadda, R. (2013). Forensic evaluations in psychiatry.*Indian Journal of Psychiatry*, *55*(4).doi: 10.4103/0019-5545.120558

Channaveerachari, N. K., Manjunatha, N., Mukesh, J., Damodharan, D., &Dass, G. P. (2022).The psychiatrist as an expert witness.*Indian Journal of Psychiatry*, 64(Suppl 1), S42-S46. https://journals.lww.com/indianjpsychiatry/fulltext/202

2/03001/The_Psychiatrist_as_an_Expert_Witness.9.aspx

Chen, Y. Y., Chen, C.-Y., & Hung, D. L. (2014). Assessment of psychiatric disorders among sex offenders: Prevalence and associations with criminal history. *Criminal Behaviour and Mental Health*, 26(1).doi: 10.1002/cbm.1926

Chung, D. S., Moon, D. S., Lee, M. H., &Kwack, Y. S. (2020).Custody Evaluation Process and Report Writing.*Journal of the Korean Academy of Child and Adolescent Psychiatry*, 31(2).doi: 10.5765/jkacap.200006

Ciardha, C. Ó.,Attard-Johnson, J., &Bindemann, M. (2017). Latency-based and psychophysiological measures of sexual interest show convergent and concurrent validity. *Archives of Sexual Behavior*, 47(3). https://pmc.ncbi.nlm.nih.gov/articles/PMC5834571/

Collins, K., Hinkebein, G., &Schorgl, S. (2020). *The John Hinckley trial & its effect on the insanity defense*. Umkc.edu. http://law2.umkc.edu/faculty/projects/ftrials/hinckley/hinckleyinsanity.htm

Dahl, Ta. (2024, October 15). *Forensic vs. clinical psychology: Understanding the differences*. Orange County

Forensics. https://www.drtdahl.com/post/forensic-vs-clinical-psychology-understanding-the-differences

Dalal P. K. (2020). Consent in psychiatry - concept, application & implications. *The Indian Journal of Medical Research*, 151(1), 6–9. doi: 10.4103/ijmr.IJMR_1518_19

De Looff, P. C., Noordzij, M. L., Nijman, H. L., Goedhard, L., Bogaerts, S., &Didden, R. (2024).Putting the usability of wearable technology in forensic psychiatry to the test: A randomized crossover trial. *Frontiers in Psychiatry*, *15*.doi: 10.3389/fpsyt.2024.1330993/full

Derflinger, B., Niedermier, J., &Misquitta, D. (2021).Use of telepsychiatry to increase resident exposure to forensic psychiatry during COVID-19. *Academic Psychiatry*, *45*(5), 662–663. doi: 10.1007/s40596-021-01457-4

Dickson-Gomez, J., Spector, A., Krechel, S., Li, J., Montaque, H. D. G., Ohlrich, J., Galletly, C., & Weeks, M. (2022). Barriers to drug treatment in police diversion programs and drug courts: A qualitative analysis. *American Journal of Orthopsychiatry*, *92*(6).doi: 10.1037/ort0000643

Disla de Jesus, V., Liem, A., Borra, D., &Appel, J. M. (2022). Who's the boss? Ethical dilemmas in the treatment of children and adolescents.*Focus*, 20(2).doi: 10.1176/appi.focus.20210037

Doak, J., Jackson, J., Saunders, C., Wright, D., Fariñas, B., &Durdiyeva, S. (2021). *Cross-examination in criminal trials towards a revolution in best practice?A report for the Nuffield Foundation.* https://irep.ntu.ac.uk/id/eprint/44924/1/1497281_Doak.pdf

Drogin, E. Y., & Barrett, C. L. (2012).*Civil competencies*.Handbook of Psychology, Forensic Psychology, 11, 295.

Eastman, N., Green, T., Latham, R., &Lyall, M. (2013). *Handbook of forensic psychiatric practice in capital cases*.The Death Penalty Project. https://www.deathpenaltyproject.org/wp-content/uploads/2013/02/DPP-Forensic-Psychiatry-Report.pdf

Faller, K. C. (2021).Forensic interviewing. In *Handbook of Interpersonal Violence and Abuse across the Lifespan: A project of the National Partnership to End Interpersonal Violence across the Lifespan (NPEIV)* (pp. 1555-1578). Cham: Springer International Publishing.doi: 10.1007/978-3-319-89999-2_266

Farahany N. A. (2016). Neuroscience and behavioral genetics in US criminal law: An empirical analysis. *Journal of Law and the Biosciences*, *2*(3), 485–509. doi: 10.1093/jlb/lsv059

Farrukh, T., &Samejo, I. A. (2024). Mental health and criminal responsibility: A critical analysis of the insanity defense. *Siazga Research Journal*, 3(2), 203–211. doi: 10.58341/srj.v3i2.81

Fazel, S., &Baillargeon, J. (2011).The health of prisoners.*The Lancet, 377*(9769), 956–965. doi: 10.1016/S0140-6736(10)61053-7

Fazel, S., Ramesh, T., &Hawton, K. (2017). Suicide in prisons: An international study of prevalence and contributory factors. *The Lancet Psychiatry, 4*(12), 946–952. https://www.thelancet.com/journals/lanpsy/article/PIIS2215-0366(17)30430-3/fulltext

Ferranti, J. (2017). Fitness for duty assessments: Teaching forensic psychiatry fellows best practices in workplace safety consultation. *Academic Psychiatry*, 41(6), 798–802. doi: 10.1007/s40596-017-0816-z

Fovet, T., Mundt, A. P., &Fazel, S. (2024). Psychiatry in prisons and corrections.*Tasman'sPsychiatry*.doi: 10.1007/978-3-030-51366-5_103

Franke, I., Speiser, O., Dudeck, M., &Streb, J. (2020). Clinical ethics support services are not as well-established in forensic psychiatry as in general psychiatry. *Frontiers in Psychiatry*, 11.doi: 10.3389/fpsyt.2020.00186

Gkotsi, G. M., Gasser, J., & Moulin, V. (2019). Neuroimaging in criminal trials and the role of psychiatrists expert witnesses: A case study. *International Journal of Law and Psychiatry*, *65*.doi: 10.1016/j.ijlp.2018.05.007

Glancy, G. D., Chatterjee, S., & Miller, D. (2021).Ethics, empathy, and detached concern in forensic psychiatry.*Journal of the American Academy of Psychiatry and the Law Online*, 49(2).doi: 10.29158/JAAPL.200106-20

Glannon, W. (2014).The limitations and potential of neuroimaging in the criminal law. *The Journal of Ethics*, *18*, 153-170. doi: 10.1007/s10892-014-9169-y

Gold, L. H., &Frierson, R. L. (Eds.).(2017). *The American Psychiatric Association publishing textbook of forensic psychiatry*.American Psychiatric Pub.

Goldyne, A. J. (2007). Minimizing the influence of unconscious bias in evaluations: A practical guide. *Journal-American Academy of Psychiatry and the Law*, *35*(1), 60.https://jaapl.org/content/35/1/60

Golumbeck, C. T. (2013). *Legal and forensic medicine in clinical psychiatry*.Springer, Berlin, Heidelberg.https://doi.org/10.1007/978-3-642-32338-6_37

Gordon, S. (2016). *Crossing the line: Daubert, dual roles, and the admissibility of forensic mental health testimony*.ScholarlyWorks.https://scholars.law.unlv.edu/facpub/969?utm_source=scholars.law.unlv.edu%2Ffacpub%2F969&utm_medium=PDF&utm_campaign=PDFCoverPages

Gottfried, E., Carbonell, J., & Miller, L. (2014).The impact of judge–defendant communication on mental health court outcomes.*International Journal of Law and Psychiatry, 37*(3).doi: 10.1016/j.ijlp.2013.11.023

Gowda, G. S., Enara, A., Ali, F., Gowda, M. R., Basavarajappa, C., Kumar, C. N., & Math, S. B. (2020).Approach to informed consent in telepsychiatric service: Indian perspective. *Indian Journal of Psychological Medicine*, *42*(5_suppl).doi: 10.1177/0253717620959781

Green, J., Bagge, A. S. L., Olausson, S., Andiné, P., Wallinius, M., &Karlén, M. H. (2023).Implementing clinical guidelines for co-occurring substance use and major mental disorders in Swedish forensic psychiatry: An exploratory, qualitative interview study with mental health care staff.*Journal of Substance Abuse Treatment, 144*.doi: 10.1016/j.jsat.2022.108899

Grisso, T. (2006). *Evaluating competencies: Forensic assessments and instruments* (Vol. 16). Springer Science & Business Media.

Grossi, L. M. (2017). Sexual offenders, violent offenders, and community reentry: Challenges and treatment considerations. *Aggression and Violent Behavior*, 34, 59–67. doi: 10.1016/j.avb.2017.04.005

Guo, H., Zhong, S., Yue, Y., Gou, N., Sun, Q., Liang, X., Wang, F., Lu, J., Li, Q., Zhou, J., & Wang, X. (2021). Self-harm history, anxiety-depression, severity of disease, and insight are significantly associated with suicide risk in forensic psychiatric inpatients of China. *Frontiers in Psychiatry*, 12.doi: 10.3389/fpsyt.2021.706416

Gutheil, T. G. (2005). The history of forensic psychiatry.*Journal of the American Academy of Psychiatry and the Law Online*, *33*(2), 259–262. https://jaapl.org/content/33/2/259

Hancq, E. S., South, K., &Vencel, M. (2021, March). Dual diagnosis: Serious mental illness and co-occurring substance.

https://tac2.nonprofitsoapbox.com/storage/documents/T

AC_Co-occuring_Evidence_Brief_March_2021_Final.pdf

Haugom, E. W., Ruud, T., &Hynnekleiv, T. (2019). Ethical challenges of seclusion in psychiatric inpatient wards: a qualitative study of the experiences of Norwegian mental health professionals. *BMC Health Services Research*, 19(1).doi: 10.1186/s12913-019-4727-4

Heilbrun, K. (2006). *Principles of forensic mental health assessment.*Oxford University Press. https://books.google.com/books?hl=en&lr=&id=CjvtBwAAQBAJ&oi=fnd&pg=PR3&dq=Principles+of+forensic+mental+health+assessment.+Oxford+University+Press.&ots=3rbLOZqv3q&sig=GSNN0OqaeKYzXvoh_qjbycHXQu4

Helmus, L. M., &Quinsey, V. L. (2020).*Predicting violent reoffending with the VRAG-R: Overview, controversies, and future directions for actuarial risk scales*. The Wiley Handbook of What Works in Violence Risk Management: Theory, Research and Practice, 119-144. doi: 10.1002/9781119315933.ch6

Hiriscau, E., Stingelin-Giles, N., Wasserman, D., & Reiter-Theil, S. (2016). Identifying ethical issues in mental health research with minors adolescents: Results of a delphi study. *International Journal of Environmental*

Research and Public Health, 13(5).doi: 10.3390/ijerph13050489

Howes, O. D., Thase, M. E., &Pillinger, T. (2021). Treatment resistance in psychiatry: State of the art and new directions. *Molecular Psychiatry*, 27(1).doi: 10.1038/s41380-021-01200-3

Hugaboom, D. (2013). The different duties and responsibilities of clinical and forensic psychologists in legal proceedings.*The Review: A Journal of Undergraduate Student Research*, 5(1), 26–32. https://fisherpub.sjf.edu/ur/vol5/iss1/4/

James, D. J., & Glaze, L. E. (2006). Mental health problems of prison and jail inmates (NCJ 213600).*U.S. Department of Justice, Bureau of Justice Statistics*.https://bjs.ojp.gov/content/pub/pdf/mhppji.pdf

Jayadi, T. I., Suharyana, T., Amanda, V., &Jaleel, B. (2024). Decoding deception: Advanced fMRI and machine learning techniques for detecting malingered psychiatric symptoms in forensic evaluations in Indonesia. *Sriwijaya Journal of Forensic and Medicolegal*, *2*(2), 151-161. https://phlox.or.id/index.php/SJFM/article/view/200

Kafka, M. (2012).Axis I psychiatric disorders, paraphilic sexual offending and implications for pharmacological treatment.*Israel Journal of Psychiatry*, 49(4). https://www.researchgate.net/profile/Martin-Kafka/publication/236182124_Axis_I_Psychiatric_Disorders_Paraphilic_Sexual_Offending_and_Implications_for_Pharmacological_Treatment/links/0a85e53be893d571fe000000/Axis-I-Psychiatric-Disorders-Paraphilic-Sexual-Offending-and-Implications-for-Pharmacological-Treatment.pdf

Kaggwa, M. M., Chaimowitz, G., Erb, B., Prat, S., Davids, A., Moulden, H. M., Robbins, A. R., John, МиниМамак, &Olagunju, A. T. (2023). Self-harming behaviors and forensic system-related factors: an analysis of the Ontario review board database. *BMC Psychiatry*, 23(1).doi: 10.1186/s12888-023-05394-4

Kennedy, H. G. (2021). Models of care in forensic psychiatry.*BJPsych Advances*, 28(1), 46–59. doi: 10.1192/bja.2021.34

Khosla, V., Davison, P., Gordon, H., & Joseph, V. (2014). The interface between general and forensic psychiatry: The present day. *Advances in Psychiatric Treatment*, 20(5), 359–365. doi: 10.1192/apt.bp.109.007336

Kirschstein, M. A., Batastini, A. B., Singh, J. P., & Graf, M. (2022). Technological innovations in forensic and correctional mental health: An introduction to the special issue. *Criminal Justice and Behavior*, *50*(2), 167-174. doi: 10.1177/00938548221141610

Koch, S. L. (2025). *Communicating forensic findings: Current practices and future directions.*doi: 10.6028/nist.ir.8510sup1

Kranenburg, L., Lambregtse-van den Berg, M., &Stramrood, C. (2023). Traumatic childbirth experience and childbirth-related post-traumatic stress disorder (PTSD): A contemporary overview. *International Journal of Environmental Research and Public Health*, *20*(4).doi: 10.3390/ijerph20042775

Krishnan, N., & Ireland, J. L. (2023). Dual diagnosis in a forensic patient sample: A preliminary tripartite investigation to inform group treatment delivery for substance use. *Journal of Forensic Psychology Research and Practice*, 1–36. doi: 10.1080/24732850.2023.2281431

Kruh, I., Gowensmith, N., Alkema, A., Swenson, K., & Platt, D. (2022). Community-based remediation of juvenile competence to stand trial: A national survey. *International Journal of Forensic Mental Health*, 1–13. doi: 10.1080/14999013.2021.2007431

Kushwaha, A., Basera, D. S., Kumari, S., Sutar, R. F., Singh, V., Das, S., &Agrawal, A. (2024). Assessment of memory deficits in psychiatric disorders: A systematic literature review. *Journal of Neurosciences in Rural Practice*, *15*(2).https://pmc.ncbi.nlm.nih.gov/articles/PMC11090569/

Mario, M. (2024).*American law institute's insanity defense standard.* EBSCO Information Services, Inc.https://www.ebsco.com/research-starters/law/american-law-institutes-insanity-defense-standard

Markowitsch, H. J., &Staniloiu, A. (2011).Neuroscience, neuroimaging and the law. *Cortex*, *47*(10), 1248-1251. https://www.sciencedirect.com/science/article/pii/S0010945211002012

Martone, C. (2022). The role of a forensic psychiatrist.*Missouri Medicine*, 119(3). https://pmc.ncbi.nlm.nih.gov/articles/PMC9324712/

McCartan, K. F. (2012). The management of sexual offenders in the community: Austerity, engagement, interaction and the 'big society'. *Prison Service Journal*, 201, 39-43. https://www.crimeandjustice.org.uk/sites/default/files/PSJ%20201%2C%20Sexual%20offenders.pdf

McFadden, D., Prior, K., Miles, H., Hemraj, S., & Barrett, E. L. (2021). Genesis of change: Substance use treatment for forensic patients with mental health concerns. *Drug and Alcohol Review*, *41*(1).doi: 10.1111/dar.13344

McSherry, B. (2000). R v Stone [1999] 2 SCR 290.*Psychiatry, Psychology and Law*, *7*(2), 279–283. doi: 10.1080/13218710009524994

McSwiggan, S., Elger, B., &Appelbaum, P. S. (2017). The forensic use of behavioral genetics in criminal proceedings: Case of the MAOA-L genotype. *International Journal of Law and Psychiatry*, *50*, 17–23. doi: 10.1016/j.ijlp.2016.09.005

Milton, S. (ed.). (2020, April 13). *Treatment reports: Do's and don'ts*. Psychology Council of New South Wales. https://www.psychologycouncil.nsw.gov.au/treatment-reports-do%E2%80%99s-and-don%E2%80%99ts

Monaro, M., Bertomeu, C. B., Zecchinato, F., Fietta, V., Sartori, G., & De Rosario Martínez, H. (2021). The detection of malingering in whiplash-related injuries: A targeted literature review of the available strategies. *International Journal of Legal Medicine*, *135*(5).doi: 10.1007/s00414-021-02589-w

Ogonah, M. G. T., Seyedsalehi, A., Whiting, D., &Fazel, S. (2023). Violence risk assessment instruments in forensic psychiatric populations: A systematic review and meta-analysis. *The Lancet Psychiatry*, 10(10), 780–789. doi: 10.1016/s2215-0366(23)00256-0

Otto, R. K., DeMier, R. L., &Boccaccini, M. T. (2014). *Forensic reports and testimony: A guide to effective communication for psychologists and psychiatrists*. John Wiley & Sons.

Owoyemi, P., Salcone, S., King, C., Kim, H. J., Ressler, K. J., &Vahia, I. V. (2021). Measuring and quantifying collateral information in psychiatry: Development and preliminary validation of the McLean Collateral Information and Clinical Actionability Scale. *JMIR Mental Health*, *8*(4).doi: 10.2196/25050

Parmigiani, G., Meynen, G., Mancini, T., &Ferracuti, S. (2024). Applications of artificial intelligence in forensic mental health: opportunities and challenges. *Frontiers in Psychiatry*, *15*.doi: 10.3389/fpsyt.2024.1435219/full

Pedersen, S. H., Radovic, S., Nilsson, T., & Eriksson, L. (2025). Dual-roles and beyond: Values, ethics, and practices in forensic mental health decision-making. *Medicine Health Care and Philosophy*.doi: 10.1007/s11019-024-10247-2

Pejovic, C. (2001). Civil law and common law: Two different paths leading to the same goal. *Comparative Maritime Law*, *155*, 7.https://heinonline.org/hol-cgi-bin/get_pdf.cgi?handle=hein.journals/poredmv155&section=6

Petrik, M. L., Billera, M., Kaplan, Y., Matarazzo, B., &Wortzel, H. (2015).Balancing patient care and confidentiality: Considerations in obtaining collateral information. *Journal of Psychiatric Practice*, *21*(3), 220–224. https://doi.org/10.1097/PRA.0000000000000072

Purser, K. (2015). Assessing testamentary capacity in the 21st century: Is banks v goodfellow still relevant? *University of New South Wales Law Journal, 38*(3), 1- 37.doi: 10.3316/informit.429550016831016

Raharjanti, N. W., Wiguna, T., Purwadianto, A., Soemantri, D., Bardosono, S., Poerwandari, E. K., Mahajudin, M. S., Ramadianto, A. S., Alfonso, C. A., Findyartini, A., Nugrahadi, N. R., Lazuardi, M. Q., Subroto, P. A. M., Saroso, O. J. D. A., &Levania, M. K. (2021). Clinical reasoning in forensic psychiatry: Concepts, processes, and pitfalls. *Frontiers in Psychiatry*, 12, 1-11. doi: 10.3389/fpsyt.2021.691377

Rassin E. (2021). 'Anyone who commits such a cruel crime, must be criminally irresponsible': context effects in forensic psychological assessment. *Psychiatry,*

Psychology, and Law, *29*(4), 506–515. doi: 10.1080/13218719.2021.1938272

Ricci, V., Martinotti, G., &Maina, G. (2024). Substance-induced psychosis: Diagnostic challenges and phenomenological insights. *Psychiatry International*, *5*(4), 759–772. doi: 10.3390/psychiatryint5040052

Rix, K. J. B., & Tracy, D. K. (2018). Malingering mental disorders: Medicolegal reporting. *BJPsych Advances*, *23*(2).doi: 10.1192/apt.bp.116.015966

Robb, A. (2023). Models and methods of cost-effective child custody evaluation.*Family Court Review*, 61(4).doi: 10.1111/fcre.12755

Rocchio L. M. (2020). Ethical and professional considerations in the forensic assessment of Complex Trauma and Dissociation. *Psychological Injury and Law*, *13*(2), 124–134. doi: 10.1007/s12207-020-09384-9

Russell, K., &Darjee, R. (2013).Practical assessment and management of risk in sexual offenders.*Advances in Psychiatric Treatment*, 19(1), 56–66. doi: 10.1192/apt.bp.111.009373

Sales, C. P., McSweeney, L., Saleem, Y., &Khalifa, N. (2018). The use of telepsychiatry within forensic practice: a literature review on the use of videolink–a ten-year follow-up. *The Journal of Forensic Psychiatry &*

Psychology, *29*(3), 387-402. doi: 10.1080/14789949.2017.1396487

Schmucker, M., &Lösel, F. (2017). Sexual offender treatment for reducing recidivism among convicted sex offenders: A systematic review and meta-analysis. *Campbell Systematic Reviews*, 13(1), 1–75. doi: 10.4073/csr.2017.8

Silva, R. C., Oliva, F., Barlati, S., Perusi, G., Meattini, M., Dashi, E., ...&Minelli, A. (2024). *Childhood neglect, the neglected trauma.A systematic review and meta-analysis of its prevalence in psychiatric disorders*.PsychiatryResearch.https://www.sciencedirect.com/science/article/pii/S0165178124001665

Snider, K. M., Devereux, P. G., & Miller, M. K. (2021). Judges' emotion: An application of the emotion regulation process model. *Psychiatry, Psychology, and Law*, *29*(2), 256–273. doi: 10.1080/13218719.2021.1904454

Stein, D. J., Shoptaw, S. J., Vigo, D. V., Lund, C., Cuijpers, P., Bantjes, J., Sartorius, N., &Maj, M. (2022). Psychiatric diagnosis and treatment in the 21st century: Paradigm shifts versus incremental integration. *World Psychiatry*, *21*(3), 393–414. doi: 10.1002/wps.20998

Steinert, T., &Henking, T. (2022).Law and psychiatry—current and future perspectives.*Frontiers in Public Health*, 10.doi: 10.3389/fpubh.2022.968168

Tay, J. L., Li, Z., &Sim, K. (2022). Effectiveness of artificial intelligence methods in personalized aggression risk prediction within inpatient psychiatric treatment settings- a systematic review. *Journal of Personalized Medicine*, *12*(9). https://www.mdpi.com/2075-4426/12/9/1470

Tejani, N. (2022, August 31). Forensic report writing.*Black n' White Journal*. https://bnwjournal.com/2022/08/31/forensic-report-writing/

Testoni, I., Nencioni, I., Arbien, M., Iacona, E., Marrella, F., Gorzegno, V., Selmi, C., Vianello, F., Nava, A., Zamperini, A., &Wieser, M. A. (2021). Mental health in prison: Integrating the perspectives of prison staff. *International Journal of Environmental Research and Public Health*, 18(21).doi: 10.3390/ijerph182111254

Tomašić, L., Peček, M., &ZrnkaKovačićPetrović. (2023). Substance-induced psychosis: A narrative review. *Current Addiction Reports*.doi: 10.1007/s40429-023-00528-w

Tully, R. J., Chou, S., & Browne, K. D. (2013). A systematic review on the effectiveness of sex offender risk assessment tools in predicting sexual recidivism of adult male sex offenders. *Clinical Psychology Review*, 33(2).doi: 10.1016/j.cpr.2012.12.002

United States v. Hinckley, 525 F. Supp. 1342 (D.D.C. 1981). https://law.justia.com/cases/federal/district-courts/FSupp/525/1342/1692613/

VanDercar, A. H., & Bruce, N. B. (2021). Fitness for duty evaluations predicated on psychological data. *Journal of the American Academy of Psychiatry and the Law Online*, 49(4).doi: 10.29158/JAAPL.210127L2-21

Van Es, R. M. S., Kunst, M. J. J., & de Keijser, J. W. (2020). Forensic mental health expert testimony and judicial decision-making: A systematic literature review. *Aggression and Violent Behavior*, *51*, 1- 14.doi: 10.1016/j.avb.2020.101387

Van Le, D., Montgomery, J., Kirkby, K. C., &Scanlan, J. (2018).Risk prediction using natural language processing of electronic mental health records in an inpatient forensic psychiatry setting. *Journal of Biomedical Informatics*, *86*, 49-58. https://www.sciencedirect.com/science/article/pii/S153204641830162X

Walczyk, J. J., Sewell, N., &DiBenedetto, M. B. (2018).A review of approaches to detecting malingering in forensic contexts and promising cognitive load-inducing lie detection techniques. *Frontiers in psychiatry*, *9*, 700.doi: 10.3389/fpsyt.2018.00700

Wang, S. B., Wang, Y. Y., Ungvari, G. S., Ng, C. H., Wu, R. R., Wang, J., & Xiang, Y. T. (2017). The MacArthur Competence Assessment Tools for assessing decision-making capacity in schizophrenia: A meta-analysis. *Schizophrenia Research*, *183*, 1-8. https://www.sciencedirect.com/science/article/pii/S0920996416305126

Wasser, T. (Ed.).(2017). *Psychiatry and the Law*.Springer International Publishing.doi: 10.1007/978-3-319-63148-6

Wathen, D. E. (2005).When the court speaks: Effective communication as part of judging. *Maine Law Review*, 57(2), 450-462.

Yohananoff, A. (2016, April 5). *The use of collateral sources in forensic evaluations: Part I*. NYC Forensics. https://www.nycforensics.com/2016/04/the-use-of-collateral-sources-in-forensic-evaluations-part-i/

www.ingramcontent.com/pod-product-compliance
Lightning Source LLC
LaVergne TN
LVHW022157200926
848481LV00006B/1773